ANCIENT CULTURE AND SOCIETY

EARLY GREECE

The Bronze and Archaic Ages

ANCIENT CULTURE AND SOCIETY

General Editor
M. I. FINLEY

*

EARLY GREECE
The Bronze and Archaic Ages

M. I. FINLEY

*Master of Darwin College and Professor Emeritus
of Ancient History in the University of Cambridge*

New and Revised Edition

W · W · NORTON & COMPANY
New York · London

CONTENTS

FIGURES

MAPS

PLATES

To
Robert Cook
and
Geoffrey Kirk

CHRONOLOGICAL TABLE

Note: All dates are B.C., and, except for a few at the end, they are all approximate.

	Date	Greece	Crete	Cyclades	Troy	Cyprus
	40,000	definite human occupation				
Neolithic	6000	Nea Nikomedeia	Cnossus			Khirokitia
	4000			Saliagos		
Bronze Age	3000	Early Helladic I / II / III	Early Minoan I / II / III	Early Cycladic	I / II / III–V / VI	Early Cypriot
	2000	Middle Helladic	Middle Minoan	Middle Cycladic		Middle Cypriot
	1600/1550	Late Helladic I	Late Minoan I	Late Cycladic	VI	Late Cypriot
	1500	II	II			
	1450		IIIA			
	1400	IIIA				
	1300	IIIB	IIIB		VIIA	
	1200	IIIC	IIIC		VIIB	

Salamis founded

Dark Age	1100	Protogeometric pottery
	1050	
	900	Geometric pottery
	800	Phoenician alphabet
	776	Olympic Games instituted
	750	Western 'colonization' begins
	650	'Colonization' begins around Black Sea
	630	Cylon's attempted *coup* in Athens
	621	Draco's codification
Archaic Age	594	Archonship of Solon
	545–	Tyranny of Peisistratids
	510	
	520–	Cleomenes I king of Sparta
	490	
	508	Cleisthenes reforms Athenian constitution
	490–	Persian Wars
	479	

Acknowledgements

The author and publishers are grateful to the following for permission to quote from copyright material: Clarendon Press, Oxford, for C. M. Bowra: *Pindar*; Cambridge University Press for G. S. Kirk and J. E. Raven: *The Presocratic Philosophers*; William Heinemann Ltd and Harvard University Press for the *Loeb Classical Library* edition of Hesiod: *Works and Days* translated by H. G. Evelyn-White.

Figure 1 is reproduced from Sir Arthur Evans: *The Palace of Minos* by permission of the Trustees of the Sir Arthur Evans Estate; Figure 3 from Marinatos: *Geras Keramopoulou* by permission of Myrtides, Athens; Figures 4a and 4b from Wace and Stubbings: *A Companion to Homer* by permission of Macmillan. Figure 2 is based on tables in J. Chadwick: *The Decipherment of Linear B*, Cambridge University Press, and in L. H. Jeffrey: *The Local Scripts of Archaic Greece*, Clarendon Press, Oxford. Figure 4d is reproduced by permission of the Agora Museum, Athens. Figure 4c is after Furtwangler-Losche and Figure 4e after Wide.

Plates Ia and Ic are reproduced by courtesy of the Ashmolean Museum, Oxford; Plate Ib the National Museum, Athens; Plates IIa and III Hirmer Verlag, Munich; Plate IIc Lord William Taylour; Plates IIb and IV the German Institute, Athens.

PREFACE

Anyone who essays a synoptic account of the ancient Greek world in the Bronze and Archaic periods, for which the largest part of the evidence is archaeological, knows that he will have to reexamine the data within a few years. Such is the tempo and increasing sophistication of archaeological work in this field. This is my third attempt: the first was in two chapters I wrote for the *Fischer Weltgeschichte*, volumes 3 (1966) and 4 (1967), published in German; the second was the original edition of the present book (1970). Considerable rewriting has again proved necessary, especially in the Bronze Age section.

In so far as there is a distinction between history and archaeology, this book is a *history* of early Greece (I do not say 'narrative' because that is impossible). In no sense is this an archaeological survey: there is no catalogue of sites and finds, no discussion of the intricacies of pottery designs and styles. My concern has been solely with the history of a civilization (or of its component cultures) over a period of some 5000 years. Throughout I have tried to indicate the nature and limits of the underlying evidence, to be open about what we do not know and about the disagreements among experts. But I have also throughout stated my own views and my own doubts explicitly, and some of the rewriting reflects rethinking as much as the impact of new discoveries. This book, in short, is a personal account, not a repository of prevailing ideas on the subject. A selected English bibliography, emphasizing recent publications, suggests where the interested reader can find detailed studies and alternative publications.

There is hardly an aspect of early Greek history that is not currently under reexamination. Inevitably, questions of chronology appear to dominate, not for their own sake because so much else hinges on changes in dating, notably the interrelationship between different regions and cultures within an area that eventually embraced a large band from Marseilles to the Black Sea. Revised carbon-14 dating, for example, has put an end to once widely held theses about Mycenaean influences in western Europe and Britain. Nor is it any longer possible to maintain the view (never very tenable) that the Minoan civilization of Crete came to an end because of the destructive effects of the massive volcanic eruption on the island of Santorini (ancient Thera). A new study of Hittite documents appears to have undermined a once vigorously argued identification with Mycenae of some of the kings referred to in those texts. Chronology apart, the most interesting new development is the increasing attention by archaeologists to population trends and settlement patterns, again with implications that spread to other questions. These are but a few of the reconsiderations imposed on the historian by discoveries and inquiries of the past decade, enough to explain why a new edition of the book was called for.

Warm thanks are due to Paul Halstead of King's College, Cambridge, for helping me to cope with the massive volume of recent archaeological publication; again to the friends who read and criticized the manuscript of the first edition—A. Andrewes, R. M. Cook, M. C. Greenstock and G. S. Kirk; and to my wife for her continuous assistance.

M. I. F.

June 1980

A NOTE ON PROPER NAMES

No effort has been made to be rigidly consistent in Angliciz-
ing Greek proper names, whether of persons or of places.
Where modern place-names are noticeably different from
the ancient, I have given the equivalents at the first occur-
rence and again in the index. Bronze Age place-names are
often unknown. The use of later Greek names should not be
taken as an indication that the same names were already in
use in the earlier ages; it can sometimes be demonstrated
that this was in fact not the case, and there are a few examples, indicated in the chapter on Crete, where the only
available method of identification is the use of a modern
name.

Part One

THE BRONZE AGE

Introduction

In the study of man's early history, what is observed most clearly and readily is his technological progress. That is why it has been a long-standing convention to divide early history into broad periods according to the hard materials from which cutting tools and weapons were fashioned—stone, copper, bronze, iron, in that order. Then, as knowledge of the past increased, the long periods were sub-divided in different ways. When it was noticed, for example, that in due course the technique of giving a sharp edge to flint and other stones normally changed from flaking to grinding, the Stone Age was divided into Old (Palaeolithic) and New (Neolithic). Soon it became necessary to speak of Lower, Middle and Upper (or Advanced) Palaeolithic; of an 'in-between' Mesolithic period; of Early and Late Bronze, and so on; and also to separate each age according to region or civilization.

A shorthand was thus created, and its use persists despite a growing awareness of its inadequacy, and even of its tendency to mislead. Copper, for example, was already in use in Neolithic Greece perhaps a thousand years before the conventional date for the beginning of the Bronze Age; and metals did not come into common use for tools and weapons for another thousand years after 3000 B.C. Furthermore, wood, bone, potting clay, skins and textiles were no less important materials, but they are not all durable enough to survive till our day; their use crossed the stone-bronze-iron evolutionary line and they must be ignored in the conventional scheme. Furthermore, profound changes in the economy, the social structure and political power occurred *inside* traditional ages: it is now agreed, for example, that the fundamental division between the Palaeolithic and the Neolithic was marked by the introduction of agriculture, not by a change in the way of manipulating flint. And, finally, there were very different time-scales in technological and social progress among different regions of Europe and western Asia, not to mention the other continents.

When all that is said (and more will be said later), the fact remains that some such convention is necessary in the attempt to give an account of the thousands of years of prehistory. Before any particular civilization discovered the art of writing and then made use of it to record its activities, beliefs and history, the modern student has only archaeological evidence, material remains, to work with. He has no linguistic or national groupings, no royal dynasties or forms of government, no revolutions or wars to use as labels. Nor would it be meaningful to divide the period from 40,000 to 4000 B.C. by centuries. Not before about 3000 B.C. does prehistory end in Mesopotamia (modern Iraq) and Egypt, about 2000 B.C. in Asia Minor and Syria, about 1000 B.C. in Greece, still later everywhere else further west. More correctly, those are the dates, in very round numbers, when prehistory shades into history. The employment (and survival) of writing was for a long time so restricted that archaeological evidence remains essential, often predominant.

In Greece the Bronze Age began about or soon after 3000 B.C. Until recently there was widespread agreement that the art of metallurgy had spread to Greece from further east. Now, however, it has been established that central European metallurgy was sufficiently ancient to provide an alternative source for its diffusion. Some prehistorians, finally, prefer the hypothesis of independent invention within the Aegean world, but I do not find that persuasive.

Whether or not migrations into Greece were involved is uncertain and also much debated: the pendulum has swung from excessive reliance on migration as an explanation of cultural innovation to total rejection. Migrations are clearly not *required* to explain the arrival of metals, but that they were possible is not subject to doubt: the Aegean Sea was a highway over which men and ideas travelled even in earliest Neolithic times (and perhaps long before). Some, at least, of the cultivated grains and domesticated animals which mark the opening of the Neolithic Age were

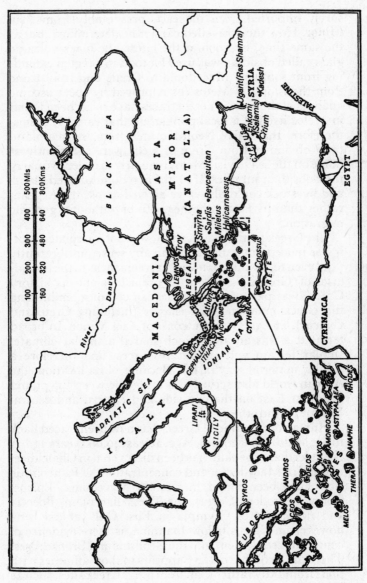

1 THE AEGEAN WORLD IN THE BRONZE AGE

surely imported from the east, presumably from Asia Minor. How they travelled cannot be determined, but at the same time, by 6000 at the latest, the black volcanic glass called obsidian was used for tools in a region extending from southern Macedonia to Crete, and it all came from the island of Melos (as is proved by spectroscopic analysis of the finds). Yet no traces have so far been found in Melos itself of a local population that early. It seems, therefore, that early Neolithic men from the mainland (and obviously from Crete as well) were sufficiently at home on the sea to visit Melos regularly in order to quarry their obsidian supplies. If so, the first domesticated plants and livestock could also have arrived across the Aegean, rather than by land, whether with or without a genuine migration.

The Greek peninsula, in short, was not an isolated unit; it was indeed not a unit at all, in any sense, until recently (and even today there is no firm agreement as to the boundaries of 'Greece'). In both its prehistory and its history Greece was part of a larger Aegean complex, embracing the Greek mainland, the islands (including Crete and Cyprus), and the western coast of Asia Minor. In broad terms this was an area which shared a similar climate, similar terrain and similar resources, and therefore a similar material way of life. Because of its location, the Aegean world also served as a bridge between Egypt and the Near East on the one side and eastern and central Europe on the other.

Human occupation of Greece has now been traced back to the Middle Palaeolithic Age, at least 40,000 years ago. A Neanderthal-type skull has been discovered in Chalcidice, in Eastern Macedonia, and concentrations of Palaeolithic sites have been found in western Macedonia, Epirus, Corcyra (modern Corfu), the Thessalian plain, Boeotia and northwest of Olympia in Elis. Only at one site, however, in Epirus below Ioannina, is there evidence of continuous settlement into the Neolithic and Bronze Ages. There the Neolithic pottery appears to show affinities with finds from Italy rather than from other Greek sites, such as Nea Nikomedeia in Macedonia (though this is admittedly a subjective impression). Nearly all these discoveries have been made since the late 1950s, so that it would be foolhardy at present to generalize about the extent of the Greek Palaeolithic remains or to discuss origins and connexions. No Palaeolithic remains have been found at Nea Nikomedeia for example, where about 6000 there was a settlement which cultivated wheat, barley, lentils and peas, which kept sheep, pigs, goats and cattle, which manufactured baskets and four different styles of pottery. Nea Nikomedeia seems to have begun life with the whole gamut of new arts whereas some early Neolithic settlements, such as Sesklo in Thessaly and Cnossus in Crete, went through a brief pre-pottery phase. Every new excavation supplies further variations and puzzles, demonstrating again and again that variation within the general Greek (not to mention the Aegean) complex is an essential part of its prehistory, though the explanations escape us, as they must when we are wholly dependent on material objects for our information.

So widespread are the known early Neolithic sites where pottery was being manufactured and agriculture practised, that it is tempting to postulate that these fundamental innovations were linked in Greece with a migration (or migrations). These first settlements were small, numbering their inhabitants in the hundreds, if that many: Cnossus apparently began with fewer on a site of less than half a hectare and their houses were single-roomed buildings scattered within the village area, unlike the dense, closely packed villages of the Near East. The next three thousand years then witnessed a considerable growth of population, demonstrated by the spread of habitation to new areas and by the greater thickness of settlement on older sites. There was growth and development in a number of ways, in the proliferation of varieties of food, in the refinement and further specialization of tools and weapons, of pottery and its decoration, of transport and architecture. If the inferences which have been drawn from other early and better known agricultural communities are valid, there was also some division of labour (not possible among hunting, food-gathering societies) and the beginnings of social stratification. And there were irreversible changes in the physical environment, not all of them necessarily favourable in the long run, caused by clearing of forests, by persistent cropping and grazing.

The so-called Early Bronze Age, as we have seen, was not marked by substantial practical application of the long-existing knowledge of metallurgy. Objects of metal continued to be rarities in the Aegean; in some areas, such as Crete, they have scarcely been found at all. The majority, whether of copper, bronze, lead or silver, were either weapons, decorative pieces, or objects perhaps connected with religion. Metal tools were hardly in evidence, and then only for the craftsman, not for the farmer. In short, metal began, and had a considerable life, as a luxury in the Aegean world, presumably available only to a wealthier social class that had arisen during the preceding Neolithic period. Stone, fired clay, bone and wood continued to be the hard materials (and it is worth reminding ourselves that they were never wholly displaced), until, finally, at the end of the third millennium, there was a rather sharp increase throughout the Aegean, not only in the quantity of metal being used but also in the scale of its employment in production.

The coming of the true age of metals introduced radically new problems. A society which *depends* on metals, even partially, has to find a place in its social structure for specialists to a degree not required before, and it must concern itself, actively and continuously, with procurement of these scarce raw materials. The Aegean world is poor in metals. For the restricted needs of the first Aegean metallurgists, scattered small local deposits would perhaps have been sufficient; a few have been tracked down in modern surveys, but by no means in all districts where metal artifacts have been found. As demand grew, it became necessary to import tin and copper (and, to look ahead, iron). The major sources of tin are a mystery today (despite confident assertions by some scholars),[1] whereas copper and iron were available in widely scattered regions

[1] See R. Maddin *et al.*, 'Tin in the Ancient Near East: Old Questions and New Finds', *Expedition* 19 (1977) 35–47.

of Europe and Asia. Transport of these metals over long distances was a feature of ancient society, and the importance of certain settlements can be explained by their location on a metal route. Thus, the attractive suggestion has been made that the early prosperity of Troy, where metallurgy was already practised in the first phase, may be attributed to its position as a bridgehead for metal transport between the lower Danube, the Aegean world and Asia Minor.

The rapid development of local metallurgical industries can be demonstrated for many Aegean sites, sometimes by deposits of slag and other direct traces of actual workshops, more often by variations in the style and technique of the finished products. The extensive intra-Aegean trade is equally well attested archaeologically, in marked contrast to the preceding centuries. The villages and hamlets of still earlier days now have a more solid 'urban' look about them, sometimes with fortification walls of stone, sited by preference on low hills or knolls near the sea or near inland lakes. But that is the only available hint that the increased wealth, the greater specialization and the various requirements of foreign trade for metals together had a significant effect on the organization and class structure of society. Nor is there even a hint about the political relations between communities.

It is tempting to try to fill the gaps in our knowledge from the more or less contemporary developments in Egypt or Mesopotamia—but that is a temptation which must be firmly resisted. It requires no more than a glance at the archaeological record to see how rapidly and totally the civilizations of the Near East had outstripped those of the Aegean in scale and complexity, both of individual communities (and of the things they built) and soon of the extension of power from the single communities outward. Not even Troy is a proper exception; one must come down to the great Cretan palaces, after 2000 B.C., before one finds anything really grandiose in the Aegean world.[1] And

[1] To help fix the scale, Stuart Piggott, *Ancient Europe* (Edinburgh University Press; Chicago, Aldine Press, 1965), p. 122, has made the following interesting calculations: Troy II would fit inside the earthwork

above all there is the absence of any form of writing. Then, when writing finally made its appearance in Greece and Crete, its spread was slow and incomplete (never reaching Troy, for example) and its employment was so restricted that it is proper to speak of Greek prehistory, rather than history, even for the centuries in which the Linear A and B scripts (discussed in Chapters 4 and 5) were being used for palace records.

Non-literacy is a severe enough limitation on the society itself. For the modern historian it is crippling. The 'events' in the whole of Aegean prehistory can be counted on one's fingers; they are known only from very much later myths and traditions, and, as we shall see, they are highly problematical at best. Archaeology reveals cataclysms, but it cannot tell us the circumstances or even who the participants were, although in a few significant instances wide-ranging inferences can be drawn with considerable probability. Individual personalities are similarly lacking, not only because of the nature of the few written texts but also because of the remarkable absence of monumental portrayal. There are no beautifully inscribed obelisks, no individualized statues or wall-paintings, whether in palaces or tombs, in any way comparable with those of the ubiquitous rulers, nobles, warriors, scribes, priests and gods of the Near East. The rulers of Cnossus and Mycenae and Troy neglected to memorialize themselves. One is free to believe if one wishes that King Minos of Cnossus, Agamemnon of Mycenae and Priam of Troy were historical personages, not figures of myth; no one has found them on the spot in any shape whatsoever, not even as a name on a slab or a seal-stone.

A by-product of all these negatives is a severe frustration and uncertainty about the chronology. There is not a single dated object from the Aegean world which is not an import (and there are precious few of those). All dates are archaeological. Relative chronology is first established

circle of the first phase of Stonehenge; the Middle Minoan palace of Mallia in Crete is about the same size as the Roman villa at Woodchester in Oxfordshire; the palace at Pylos is about as large in area as the Iron Age settlement at Glastonbury in Somerset.

from the stylistic evolution of pottery and the strata or layers within the ruins on each individual site. The pivots, the 'absolute' dates, are then fixed by synchronizations, made possible by imported and exported objects, with a few known dates from Egypt or Syria. And finally the time between any two 'pivots' is divided according to the quantity of objects recovered and the extent of stylistic change. Architectural developments provide a further check.

The most serious weakness is the impossibility of fixing precisely enough the tempo of change either in styles and techniques of pottery and other objects or in the stratification. A margin of error must always be allowed, even in the new scientific tests, such as carbon-14, and though a margin of a hundred years may seem trifling when we are dealing with a millennium or more, it amounts to three full human generations.[1] Hence an error of that magnitude can create false ideas about growth or change or migration, and the risks are multiplied whenever two or more cultures are brought into relation with each other. Therefore, when archaeologists produce dates as precise as 1440 or 1270 B.C., they are overstepping the limits of reasonableness and enveloping their calculations in a false glow of certainty.

Once the limits are understood, approximate dates are useful and indeed indispensable. The Bronze Age section of the chronological table opening this volume gives a synchronization for Greece, Crete, Cyprus and Troy. No greater claim is made for it than that it represents a scheme which many archaeologists would accept as reasonable in the present state of knowledge. By a harmless convention, the periods in Greece are called *Helladic*, in Crete *Minoan*, and in the central Aegean islands *Cycladic*. By another convention there is a further breakdown into double triads:

---

[1] Currently, 'raw' carbon-14 dates require complex adjustments, about which there is no complete agreement; see C. Renfrew, *Before Civilization: The Radiocarbon Revolution and Prehistoric Europe* (London: Jonathan Cape, 1973). For the period and subject-matter of this book, the contribution of carbon-14 dating is still minimal and I have thought it less misleading not to employ it.

Early, Middle and Late, each sub-divided into I, II and III. That may create an aesthetically pleasing pattern, despite the unevenness of tempo among Helladic, Minoan and Cycladic, and one can sometimes detect a fairly clear beginning, middle and end. On the other hand, the triadic system has insufficient warrant in many sites, and it has led to rather violent methods in the attempt to force the increasing and unwilling evidence into a frame which was created in the early days of Aegean archaeology. For individual sites, the preferable procedure is that adopted by the excavators at Troy and elsewhere of numbering each phase in turn, beginning with I and continuing as necessary. For larger areas, a more general scheme is desirable; the conventional triads have been retained for reference purposes in this volume, since no alternative is available at present.

2

The 'Coming of the Greeks'

THE weakness of the conventional, excessively symmetrical division of the Bronze Age into triads and subtriads becomes apparent when it is recognized that the sharpest and most widespread break in the archaeological record occurs between Early Helladic II and III, rather than at the beginning of Early Helladic I or in the transition from Early to Middle Helladic, usually placed early in the second millennium B.C. Towards the close of the third millennium (as determined by pottery finds), heavy destruction is visible in a number of major sites in the Argolid—Lerna, Tiryns, Asine, Zygouries, probably Corinth—and Attica, and the Cyclades seem to have suffered too. Precisely how widespread the devastation may have been in Greece is still not determined. It was not universal, but one can hardly dismiss as coincidence the fact that burning and destruction in the final century or so of the third millennium are also in evidence across the Aegean, in Troy II, further south at Beycesultan near the headwaters of the Meander River, and in many other sites, even in Palestine.

The word 'break' should be understood in its strongest sense. Archaeological records are filled with changes of all kinds, but not often with anything so massive and abrupt, so widely dispersed, as occurred at this particular time. In Greece nothing comparable was to happen again until the end of the Bronze Age a thousand years later. Settlements which were, for their time, rich and powerful, and which had had a long history of stability and continuity, literally came tumbling down, and what followed differed unmistakably in scale and quality. Archaeology cannot normally put names to the people or content to a disaster, but in this particular combination of disasters it is legitimate to ask whether they are not witness to the concurrent arrival on one side of the Aegean Sea of migrants who spoke an

EARLY GREECE: THE BRONZE AGE

2 BRONZE AGE GREECE

early form of Greek and, on the eastern side, of people speaking other, inter-related Indo-European languages— Hittite, Luwian, Palaic.

There is an understandable reluctance to pose the question so directly. The tendency to equate language with race has bedevilled the study of prehistory and history ever since the discovery that the languages of Europe, Asia and North Africa can be classified into 'families', primarily according to structural similarities (often to be apprehended only by expert analysis). The numerous Indo-European family includes the ancient languages of India (Sanskrit) and Persia, Armenian, the Slavic tongues, several Baltic languages (Lithuanian, for instance) Greek and Albanian, the Italic languages, among which are Latin and its modern descendants, the Celtic group, of which Gaelic and Welsh have retained some vitality to our own day, the Germanic languages, and various dead languages once spoken in the Balkans (Illyrian) or in Asia Minor (such as Hittite and Phrygian). Serious students have now abandoned the romantic (or worse) conception of an 'Indo-European race', with a characteristic temperament, manners and institutions, sweeping over the land and replacing the cultures they found with one they brought with them from some hypothetical original home. Neither in Greece nor in Asia Minor is there evidence to justify anything like that. The institutions and culture of the great Hittite empire, which in the second half of the second millennium controlled Asia Minor, and extended its influence beyond, about which we have many documents (written in the cuneiform script the Hittites adopted from Babylonia), were the products of developments within Anatolia (Asia Minor), not something fully pre-existing and brought into the area, in one piece, by a single conquering migration. Presumably the same was true of the 'coming of the Greeks', who left behind no written documents earlier than the Linear B tablets.

When that is said, however, a hard core of reality remains which must be accounted for. The time was to come, well before the end of the second millennium B.C., when much of Europe and large districts in western and central Asia spoke one or another Indo-European language. These languages were not native throughout this vast area from time immemorial, and there are sound reasons for believing that they had rivals within their own territories all through the Bronze Age (and demonstrably so into historical times in some regions). There is, in the end, no escaping the conclusion that some movement of peoples was involved; that the final linguistic map is the result not of one movement but of several, at different periods, from different centres and in different directions. A new language, unlike new technology, has never been adopted by a people without an immigration, a physical infusion of a new element into the population.

Nothing else will explain, for example, the close affinity, within the Indo-European family, between Sanskrit and Lithuanian. One of these movements seems to be reflected in the great destructions in Greece, Troy and elsewhere in Anatolia in the late third millennium B.C. There is no way at present to *prove* this hypothesis. Archaeological evidence often fails to throw any direct light on the history of languages or even on migrations which are known from other sources or from linguistic inferences. Thus the Huns have never been clearly identified in central European archaeology, but we know beyond doubt that the Huns made a devastating sweep into Europe. Our difficulties are further compounded by the unpredictable behaviour of language following a conquest. The Normans failed to impose Norman French in England, despite the thoroughness of their conquest and control, whereas Magyar (Hungarian), a member of the Ural-Altaic family, has survived to this day as a linguistic island surrounded by wholly unrelated Indo-European languages (German, Rumanian and several Slavic languages).

It is therefore necessary to define more closely what the suggestion of the appearance in the Aegean of Indo-European speakers before 2000 B.C. implies, and what it does not imply. To begin with, all racialist implications must be firmly rejected: it is absurd to imagine that they were already 'Greeks' having some mysterious affinity with the rulers of Mycenae 700 or 800 years later, not to mention Sappho or Pericles or Plato. Nor is it necessary to think that at the moment of entry they were speaking a language which could be easily recognized as Greek. More probably the Greek we know was finally fashioned in Greece itself, the idiom of the new arrivals being influenced by that of the older population of the peninsula. It emerged in the Mycenaean period at the latest (as is shown by the Linear B tablets); by then, on the evidence of later changes and variations within the language, two, or possibly three, closely related Greek dialects seem to have been diffused throughout the area. The completely articulated classical dialect pattern—Ionic, Aeolic and Doric, with their variants and sub-categories, such as Attic—must then be attributed to the period after the breakdown of the Mycenaean world, that is, after 1200 B.C. (Map 4).

Much of the complex history of the Greek language can be explained as a purely linguistic evolution. It is therefore unnecessary to postulate successive waves of Greek-speaking immigrants into Greece, each with its own dialect, which used to be widely assumed. To say that does not preclude the possibility that there were further migrations after the end of the third millennium from across the Aegean, for example, but it does not require them for the history of the language. Here we come up against the most notorious crux of all in interpreting the archaeological data. That important new culture-traits and impulses kept coming into Greece in the second millennium is evident on many sites. But how were they brought, by merchants and travelling craftsmen or by migration and conquest? The latter is the easy explanation—too easy. Two Middle Helladic innovations are worth closer consideration.

The first is the so-called Minyan ware, a characteristic style of pottery with a 'soapy' texture. It was remarkably widespread in Greece, the islands and parts of western Anatolia from the beginning of the second millennium, that is, from Middle Helladic I, and many scholars have considered it an outstanding characteristic of a new culture brought by migrants, whom some have identified with 'the Greeks'. However, wheel-made pottery has now been found at Lerna and elsewhere in Early Helladic III which cannot be distinguished in any significant way from Minyan, except that it is an earlier, more primitive variety. There is thus no need to attach the great popularity of Minyan ware in the Middle Helladic period to a migration. All the archaeological evidence taken together now argues for the earlier date, at the end of Early Helladic III.

Secondly, a new burial practice appears, widely dispersed, at the beginning of the Middle Helladic period. Shallow box-like graves (so-called cist-graves) were dug, sometimes lined with stone and strewn with pebbles, each containing a single body, and sealed with a slab. At first they tended to be so small that the bodies were placed in the contracted (or foetal) position; furthermore, no grave-goods were added. Eventually they became larger and richer. What is new is none of this—already widespread in the Cyclades centuries earlier—but the practice of placing the cist-graves of children, and occasionally of adults, within the house, under the floor or behind walls. A new outlook is indicated. But does that require a migration? If so, the new population would have had to be exceedingly numerous and all-conquering to impose a new funeral pattern so rapidly, and it is odd that cemeteries outside the village continued to be the rule for adults. The fact is that in the Aegean area throughout the Bronze Age, and in historical times as well, there was a bewildering variety of burial practices, varying regionally as well as in time, and often co-existing for long periods in the same community. Bodies were buried individually and in family groups, in different kinds of containers; they were sometimes dug up after decomposition and then the bones were re-buried; eventually cremation supplemented burial. The thinking behind the many shifts in practice usually escapes us, but one thing is certain, namely, that most of the changes arose without benefit of a migration. Hence there is no particular reason why the introduction of intramural burial should of itself imply a migration.

The Aegean was always a highway for ideas, techniques and institutions, at the beginning of the second millennium as at other times. It is a curious habit never to credit the people under consideration with any originality,

Ib Terracotta 'frying pan', 30 cm
high, showing Cycladic ship,
from Syros

Ic
Cycladic 'idol', 32 cm high, found
in Amorgos

Ia Lead ship model, 42 cm long, Naxos, probably before 2500 B.C.

IIa Late Minoan seal-stones in semi-precious stone: *left* (impression) from Praesus, 2 cm in diameter; *right* from near Cnossus, 3 cm in diameter

IIb Thin gold disk, 5 cm in diameter, shaft-grave Circle A, Mycenae

IIc Clay snake, 20 cm in diameter, Mycenae, perhaps 1300 B.C.

always to make them borrowers and someone else the inno-
vators. Anyway, originality never means creation out of
nothing, and it is no less valuable and consequential when
it starts from an idea borrowed from elsewhere. If, as
appears, the Argolid was the centre of destruction by intruders in the late third milliennium, the further implication
is that it was from this district that there eventually grew
and spread the culture of the Early Helladic III and
Middle Helladic periods out of which, in turn, there
emerged the Late Helladic (or Mycenaean) civilization.
That is a very different picture from the romantic one of the
conquest which blanketed the whole, or even most, of
Greece in one great swoop. The 'coming of the Greeks', in
other words, meant the arrival of a new element who combined with their predecessors to create, slowly, a new civilization and to extend it as and where they could.

The destruction of established settlements, such as
Lerna, did not mean that its inhabitants were killed off or
that comparable destruction took place in the hinterland.
Some places were abandoned for longer or shorter periods,
others not. Furthermore, the Bronze Age in Greece was not
restricted to a few power-centres such as Early Helladic II
Lerna or Late Helladic Mycenae. Because the number of
excavated sites is still a tiny fraction of the whole and
because archaeologists naturally try to expend their
limited time and resources on sites which promise to be
most fruitful, an illusion of grandeur results. It is a sober-
ing experience to read through a recently published catalogue of places now known to have been inhabited in the
southwestern Peloponnese. On that small space, bounded
by the Alpheus River, Mt. Taygetus, the Messenian Gulf
and the Ionian Sea, the total of Late Helladic sites may be
as high as 200, of Middle Helladic perhaps 100 on present
evidence, which is certainly incomplete. Most of them
were mere hamlets, and many were deserted for all time at
the end of the Bronze Age.[1] These figures reflect both the
'inner colonization' of Greece from various centres and a
steady increase in the absolute population figures. To

[1] W. A. McDonald and R. Hope Simpson in *American Journal of
Archaeology*, 73 (1969) 123–77.

attempt to separate newcomers from their predecessors in such a development is impossible. And similarly with their respective contributions to the newly developing culture, or better, cultural complex. In sum, everyone contributed in one way or another, including people outside the Greek peninsula, in Crete, the Cyclades and Anatolia.

Unfortunately there is little that can be said about the new culture until the sudden outburst of power and luxuriant opulence revealed by the shaft-graves at Mycenae beginning before 1600 B.C. For five or six hundred years, from the beginning of Early Helladic III right through the Middle Helladic phase, the material remains are consistently so poverty-stricken that we are left unprepared for the great age that followed. The hamlets (for even Lerna can hardly be called more than that now) have a general uniformity of aspect: usually sited on mounds or low knolls and unfortified, irregular rather than laid out, huddled, lacking palaces or other really large buildings. Metal tools and weapons were pathetic, the latter rare altogether and too precious to be expended as grave-goods. Although pottery finds suggest some contact between the Argolid and the western islands of Ithaca and Leucas, perhaps even with the Lipari islands north of Sicily, the over-all impression is one of a grey uniformity and of isolation in the Middle Helladic period. Only the appearance, almost from the beginning, of Cretan objects and Cretan influences strikes a different note: an occasional imported Cretan cup or vase is found in a mainland grave, and potters in Athens and elsewhere began to introduce Minoan shapes among their wares.

Just what these Cretan connexions signify is hard to say. There is no reason to believe in any kind of Cretan authority over Greece in the eighteenth or seventeenth century. Nothing in the poor material remains reveals the developments in social organization and in ideas which, it is reasonable to assume, lay at the foundation of the subsequent Mycenaean civilization. Only the spread of settlement and the implied growth in population, already noticed, offer a hint that something significant was happening, however slowly.

3

The Islands

THE eastern Mediterranean, unlike the western, is dotted
with islands. Except for Rhodes and Cyprus, only occasionally did they play an independent role in historical
times, if for no other reason because of their limited size and
resources. Earlier, however, when population was small
everywhere, when technology and social organization
were less advanced, there were periods during which some
of the islands (or groups of islands) were in the forefront of
important developments in civilization. Crete was eventually outstanding, but relatively behindhand in the early
metallurgical stage.

It is the Cyclades to which one must first turn. This
cluster of small islands, extending in a southeasterly direction from Ceos and Andros, close to the southern tips of
Attica and Euboea, respectively, to Thera (modern Santorini), Anaphe and Astypalaea, forms the central bridge
across the Aegean Sea between Greece and Asia. Ranging
in size from Naxos (170 square miles) to mere mounds of
rock jutting from the sea, they have a forbidding
appearance that is rather deceptive. Their coasts, inhos-
pitable to modern ships with few exceptions, are dotted
with bays suitable for Bronze Age vessels (both peaceful
and piratical). And many islands possessed arable land: it
was agriculture, fishing and the herding of sheep, goats
and pigs that sustained the bulk of the inhabitants, rather
than seafaring. On the other hand, it was seafaring,
together with stone and metal working, that gave the
Cyclades their importance in the present context. Appro-
priately enough, the most numerous of the early representations of Aegean ships have been found there—small
models in lead from Naxos (*Plate Ia*), possibly to be dated
before 2500 B.C., and engravings on flat circular terracotta

objects (irresistibly named 'frying pans' by archaeologists) from Syros (*Plate Ib*), of a slightly later date. The ships have steep prows, no sails, and about a dozen oars on each side.

The Naxian models were unnoticed for nearly thirty years after their discovery,[1] and that is sufficient indication of the archaeological neglect of the Cyclades hitherto. Apart from one flurry at the turn of the present century, systematic excavation did not begin before the late 1950s. In consequence, all conclusions and general statements must be read as preliminary and tentative. Until recently, for example, no certain evidence had existed of a Neolithic phase. Now we have some from Ceos, and more ancient finds from tiny Saliagos, off Antiparos, going back perhaps to 4000 B.C. This late Neolithic culture seems unrelated to that of Crete or the eastern Aegean but similar to finds from nearby Attica, Euboea and Corinth. However one explains the affinities, it appears that migrants crossing the sea by-passed the Cyclades for 2000 years (as we have already noticed in connexion with the exploitation of Melian obsidian), that the first settlements were few and isolated, and that there was a sudden blossoming in the Early Bronze Age, after 3000 B.C. Not surprising, influences are visible from both Greece and Asia Minor, but the Early Bronze Cycladic culture formed traits of its own which cannot be mistaken. More correctly, one should speak of Cycladic cultures; in the material sphere, which is all we know, distinctions become more prominent as the volume of evidence accumulates, showing the development of local specialities in Syros, Amorgos, Naxos and perhaps elsewhere. The so-called Keros-Syros culture, contemporary with Early Helladic II and Early Minoan II, in the centuries beginning about 2500, marked the apogee. Metallurgical techniques influenced those of Crete and Greece, as far as Epirus; metals may have been exported (at least silver and lead, relatively abundant in the Cyclades); manufactured articles in clay and marble were widely distributed. Yet there were scarcely any large

[1] See now C. Renfrew, 'Cycladic Metallurgy and the Aegean Early Bronze Age', *American Journal of Archaeology*, 71 (1967), pp. 1–20.

settlements or heavy concentrations of people. Even Phy-lakopi on Melos, the most considerable Early Bronze Cycladic community known so far, remained unfortified.

The most notable of all Cycladic products were the marble 'idols', predominantly but not exclusively female, found in large numbers in graves, not only in the islands themselves but also on the mainland of Greece and in Asia Minor. Ranging in size from a few inches to, in one or two cases, five feet, these statuettes, often quite crude, are flat from front to back, with elongated oval heads. The sexual aspects are understressed, sometimes virtually absent, and the total impression is of an almost *avant garde* geo-metrical abstractness (*Plate Ic*). They were manufactured primarily to accompany the dead in their graves, and so they reflect some religious impulse or conception, which was shared outside the limits of the Cyclades. It is idle to pretend that we can grasp the thinking, just as we cannot yet understand a later Cycladic novelty, again in the field of religion. On Ceos in the Middle Bronze Age there was a building which appears to be a temple, at a time when such structures were unknown elsewhere in the Aegean world. In the ruins have been found hundreds of fragments of life-sized hollow clay female statues, the debris of at least nine-teen individual figures, and possibly more than twenty-four. If they were goddesses, they had no known precedents in the Aegean, and few if any successors for nearly another thousand years.

By the Middle Bronze Age the Cyclades had fallen off in importance. There are no signs of major disturbance; on the contrary, the remains reveal a continuous existence right through the prehistoric period, and the historical as well. But now their smallness reduced these islands to minor significance, to be noticed only on occasion, either because of some natural advantage or in relation to some larger and greater power. Thus the marble of Naxos and Paros retained its pre-eminence for many centuries. Thera, which suffered a major volcanic catastrophe early in the Late Helladic period, nevertheless became, in the Archaic period, a centre of sufficient prominence to be res-ponsible for the first Greek settlement in Cyrene (Libya).

EARLY GREECE: THE BRONZE AGE

Naxos and Melos were destined to occupy a special place in the historian Thucydides' account of the fifth-century Athenian Empire, and, still later, Melos gave us the best known of all Greek sculptures, the 'Venus of Milo' now in the Louvre. In all significant respects, then, the history of the Cyclades was an integral part of the history of Greece, outstanding for a fleeting moment at the beginning of the Bronze Age.

Unlike the Cyclades, Cyprus was integrated into the Greek sphere only for periods, and never fully. With its 3500 square miles, it was the largest island in the eastern Mediterranean (somewhat larger than Crete), and its location linked it to Anatolia and even more to Syria, rather than to Greece. The shortest run to Asia Minor is less than fifty miles, to Syria about seventy-five, whereas Rhodes, the easternmost Greek centre, is no nearer (250 miles) than Alexandria in Egypt. Good harbours, suitable for ancient shipping if not for modern ocean-going vessels (save for Famagusta), were most numerous on the east and south coasts, pointing to the Levant. The destiny of Cyprus was therefore shaped by two factors, neither of which the Cypriots could themselves control. One was the commercial and political situation in the eastern Mediterranean as a whole. Active trade between Greece and the Levant normally benefited Cyprus as a station on the way, but wars for possession of Syria or conflicts over naval supremacy (as those between Venice and the Turks in the sixteenth century A.D.) could have destructive effects. The second factor was the extent of demand abroad for its copper ore, the key to Cypriot growth and prosperity in the Bronze Age. But one should not forget that, apart from the narrow mountain range on the north side and the extensive mountains of the west and southwest, Cyprus has not only much arable land but also good inland communications, a rarity in the Aegean. For thousands of years agriculture was the basis of Cypriot life; the substantial coastal towns did not emerge until the export of copper took on significant proportions.

The early history of population movements is obscure, not only for the usual reasons but also because of an unexplained volatility in the settlement pattern. Sites were frequently abandoned and not later re-occupied; the next inhabitants often preferred a fresh start somewhere nearby. The earliest pre-pottery Neolithic phase, soon after 6000 B.C., seems to have been thinly represented and may have been short-lived, with a hiatus in the fifth millennium. Then a second Neolithic phase appeared, with more than a hundred sites now identified.[1] The beginning of the Bronze Age in the third millennium B.C. is still hard to date properly. However, such innovations later in the millennium as new pottery shapes and burial practices, considered together with the art of metal-working in a thinly peopled country, may point to migration, conceivably coming from Asia Minor, through Morphou Bay in the northwest, as a backlash of the troubles in Anatolia mentioned at the beginning of Chapter 2.

The final centuries of the third millennium witnessed slow but steady growth, revealed by the increase in the number and size of the settlements. Most were in the interior, in agricultural regions with good supplies of water, but native copper was being mined from the start, and at least one harbour-town, later known as Citium (modern Larnaka), was immediately established on the south coast for exports (an inference from a few Egyptian finds in the ruins). After 2000, westward trade began to pick up, not with Greece but with Crete; that island now looked further afield, beyond the Cyclades, pressed by its own growing need for copper. And trade with the Levant grew as well: cuneiform texts from Mari on the Euphrates River refer to copper and bronze imports from Alasiya (commonly held to be Cyprus) in the eighteenth century. Cyprus now entered her greatest period, which continued until 1200 B.C. The interior dwindled in importance, as genuine urban centres grew all along the southern and eastern seaboard, centres of manufacture as well as of trade. The graves give abundant evidence of wealth and luxury—and also of weapons, which Cypriots could now afford to expend in this way. The eastern orientation is un-

[1] See N.P. Stanley Price, 'Khirokitia and the Initial Settlement of Cyprus', *Levant* 9 (1977) 66–89.

mistakable, until about 1400, when pottery from Mycenaean Greece began to invade the island. One calculation
will indicate the scale of this new phenomenon, which
lasted for two centuries. At the important Cypriot Bronze
Age site, near the village of Enkomi about three miles
inland from Salamis Bay on the east coast, so many large
and expensive mixing-bowls and jugs of the Mycenaean
III A type have been found that the total is comparable
with those from the rest of the Aegean world together,
including Greece itself.

The economic importance of Cyprus at this time is
clearly not in question. Unfortunately, attempts to give
something of an account of the economic activity, such as
the range of copper exports, have so far proved to be little
better than guesswork. Copper ingots, for example, are
found or pictured everywhere, in Greece, in Egypt, even in
Sardinia, and a good proportion probably came from
Cyprus, but we do not really know. The cargo of a wrecked
30-foot vessel off Cape Gelidoniya, at the southwestern
corner of Anatolia—sailing westwards about 1200 B.C.,
possibly under a Syrian captain—included at least one ton
of copper, bronze and tin, a quantity of tools and other
objects, most of them carried as scrap metal, and unidenti-
fiable perishable goods in jars.[1] The archaeologist who
excavated the wreck was understandably confident that
Cyprus was the source of the copper and the scrap metal,
but subsequent metallurgical analysis has cast serious
doubt, without indicating an alternative provenance.

The economic developments affected (and were in turn
affected by) the power structure in Cyprus in ways that
may have been comparable to those in Greece, but could
not have been possible in the small islands of the Cyclades.
The numerous weapons in the graves and the fortified
settlements and hill-forts of the interior are pointers, the
political interpretation of which rests heavily on the
identification of the place-name Alasiya. The key question
is whether or not there was some centralized control over

---

[1] For a very full account of the discovery and its implications, see G.
F. Bass *et al.*, *Cape Gelidoniya, a Bronze Age Shipwreck (Transactions of the
American Philosophical Society*, vol. 57, part 8, 1967).

the wealthy island, and if so, by whom, Cypriots or Asiatic mainlanders. The name Alasiya appears in Egyptian, Hittite, North Syrian and other Near Eastern documents throughout the second millennium, and there can no longer be serious doubt of the identification with Cyprus, or at least with as much of the island as the rulers of Enkomi controlled. The 'king of Alasiya' was a considerable figure, who could stand up to the greater and better known monarchs of the Near East. He addressed the Egyptian Pharaoh as 'my brother'. The king of Ugarit (now Ras Shamra) in northern Syria called him 'my father'. He was a nuisance, and sometimes more, to the rulers of the Hittite Empire, who managed to bring him under control for a time, but not for long, and against whom he was able to hold his own in naval warfare. 'My brother' was mere diplomatic politeness, of course, and it can hardly be imagined that Alasiya was even faintly on a level of equality with the Hittite Empire or Egypt. But it *was* a power.

After 1100 the name Alasiya disappears. The Assyrians subsequently seem to have called the island Yadnana, and eventually Cyprus replaced all other names, though we cannot date it or identify its origin. Cyprus is also the word for copper (Kupfer, cuivre) in modern European languages, but not in Greek, which adds one last complication to the story. Nothing can really be said about the languages spoken on the island in the Neolithic and Bronze Ages. There is nothing to indicate that Cyprus was penetrated by the migrations which brought Indo-European languages to Asia Minor and Greece by 2000 B.C. (If there is anything to the suggestion of a migration from Anatolia in the late third millennium, it would have been of people fleeing from the ancestors of the Hittites.) Neither Alasiya nor Yadnana nor even, so far as we can judge, Cyprus is an Indo-European name. The only writing which has turned up consists of several hundred graffiti and a few tablets found at Enkomi and in Syria (Ras Shamra), the earliest dated to about 1500 on archaeological grounds. Because the characters show clear affinity with Linear A, the script has been labelled Cypro-Minoan. However, it now appears probable that three distinct scripts are involved, and that the languages of two of them are Western Asiatic. The flood of Mycenaean ceramics between 1400 and 1200 was not accompanied by other Mycenaean culture traits and it is therefore unlikely that there was an influx of people from Greece along with the pottery.

The time was to come, however, when the Greek language was spoken and written by a large proportion of the Cypriots, and the form it took in the classical period gives the necessary clue to the date of introduction. The dialect is closely linked with that of Arcadia, the most land-locked district in the Peloponnese, and the writing was not only syllabic (when all the other Greeks had gone over to the phonetic alphabet[1]) but it retained seven signs from Linear B and others which were modifications of that extinct script. The Greek language and script were therefore established in Cyprus before the final disappearance of Mycenaean civilization, and before the Peloponnese had gone over to a West Greek dialect. In Chapter 6 we shall see that the date was about 1200, shortly before Bronze Age Cyprus was devastated, the victim, like much of Syria and Asia Minor, of the so-called 'Sea Peoples'.

[1]. In a syllabic script, most of the signs stand for syllables (a consonant and a vowel together), as in the classical Cypriot signs reproduced in Figure 2. A phonetic alphabet such as our own, in contrast, is made up for the most part of signs, each of which represents a vowel or consonantal sound.

4

The Islands

THE other great island in the eastern Mediterranean, Crete (3200 square miles), had a very different development. In modern times large areas have been forbidding and not very productive, in part at least because of mistreatment by man. If one approaches from the south, the view is rugged and spectacular, as the mountains come down to the sea. The White Mountains in the west are almost inaccessible. But in antiquity eastern and central Crete was justly famed for its meadows and pastoral uplands, its olives and vines, its oaks and cypresses, its protected beaches on the northern and eastern shores. Unlike Cyprus, however, Crete was poor in mineral resources and it was less favourably located for sea-borne traffic to and from Asia Minor, Syria and Egypt.

For more than 3000 years Crete gave no hint of what was to come in the Bronze Age. The earliest Neolithic habitations go back to abut 6000 B.C. at Cnossus, but the subsequent three millennia are poorly known. One noteworthy feature of at least the later Neolithic period was the occupation of the mountain caves with which the island is dotted: remains of human activity have been found in hundreds of them. The general impression is that Neolithic Crete lived pretty much in isolation. Melian obsidian has been found in Neolithic levels at Cnossus and Phaestus but no metal remains dating before the third millennium, and very few before about 2500 or 2300. By that time the people had increased considerably in numbers and wealth, and had made great strides in technology. The more important settlements were at the eastern end of the island (unless we are misled by the current state of Cretan archaeology), but eventually there was a shift to the centre, and there were hamlets everywhere, even in the forbidding western region.

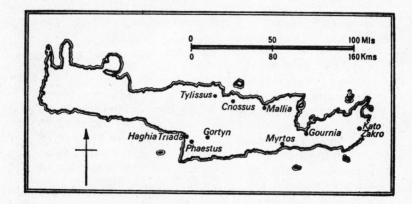

3 ANCIENT CRETE

The development from the Stone Age to the Bronze is far from clearly understood. At Cnossus, Sir Arthur Evans saw no sharp break and visualized the Early Minoan period (now thought to span the third millennium) as a long transitional one. More recently archaeologists have disputed his view, after taking account of the very different archaeological record at other sites. Evans, who first uncovered the palace at Cnossus in 1899, and then worked there with great skill and energy until his death in 1941, not surprisingly tended to impose a Cnossian stamp on the whole island. His division into periods conceals too much: Crete, like Greece, was at this time not uniform or monolithic in its culture. But Evans seems to have been right in conceiving of the Early Minoan phase as a direct evolutionary growth, not as a break from the late Neolithic culture. In many sites, the line between Early Minoan I and II, about 2500 B.C., is much more striking, as evidenced by the stone vases, rich jewelry and copper daggers of the later period. Regional variations are equally striking. For example, of the 500-odd Early Minoan II copper and bronze objects now catalogued, approximately two thirds come from the south of the island, whereas the early silver and lead artifacts, far fewer in number, were nearly all found in the north and the northeast. At a site on the south coast near the modern village of Myrtos, discovered in 1962, excavators have found large quantities of pottery, some of which provide links with contemporary deposits elsewhere in Crete, but some of which do not. More interesting, they have unearthed about one hundred clay and stone spindle whorls and loom weights, virtually no metal and some hundred blades of Melian obsidian. Occupation of the site was restricted to the Early Minoan II period, and was brought to an end by a conflagration.[1]

The discovery of an unsuspected Early Minoan settlement tucked away on the south coast opened the door to wide speculation: thus, the excavator originally suggested a 'textile centre' (which he has now abandoned). However, one may safely note that all the newer evidence helps to confirm some of the statements made earlier in this book about social development in general. The predominance of stone and clay tools long after the introduction of metallurgy is seen in the absence of metal tools for agriculture, and in the disproportion of daggers among the metal artifacts (perhaps half the total). This was linked with the development of a more ramified social structure, of specialization of labour, and of what may be called an urban component. There may also have been a trend towards specialization as between communities. The roots of these important developments lay in the Late Neolithic Age, within Crete itself, invisible though they now are to us. That is to say, although Crete had emerged from its long isolation to enter the Aegean Bronze Age complex, receiving influences from Greece and Macedonia, from the Cyclades, from Asia Minor notably, from Syria and even from Egypt (probably indirectly), the history of Crete, as we study it from its material remains, is neither one of mechanical imitation nor one of extensive immigration, but one of a society which absorbed new elements into a coherent internal development of its own.

[1] P. Warren, *Myrtos* (London 1972).

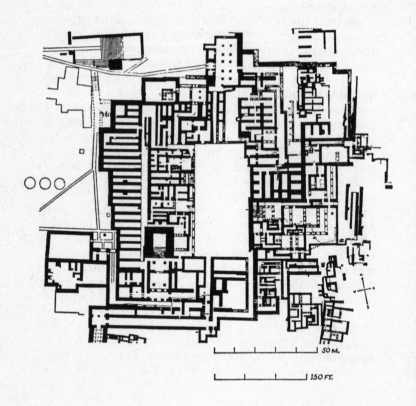

Figure 1 Palace at Cnossus

The signs of inventive originality are numerous and unambiguous. Vases and other small objects were regularly re-shaped and re-designed, not just copied, even when borrowing from abroad is most obvious. The basic techniques of metallurgy were perhaps learned from the Cyclades, including the use of arsenic as a hardening alloy for copper in the absence of tin. But the copper daggers, the most prominent of the Early Minoan metal artifacts, were peculiarly Cretan, and that is only one example. In the course of the Early Minoan period there emerged, in embryo, the unique Cretan style of architecture, with its cell-like, agglutinative structure, which was to culminate in later centuries in the palace at Cnossus, covering with its courtyards about five acres of ground (*Figure 1*). And one negative fact also deserves notice: the familiar small human statuettes of the Neolithic Age were no longer manufactured, and with them disappeared for a considerable time—until the Middle Minoan period—the display of the human form in the arts generally.

By the end of the Early Minoan period, Cretan technology had progressed nearly as far as it (or anyone else in the Aegean and the Near East) could in the Bronze Age. The Middle Minoan period which followed, the golden age of Crete, between 2000 and 1600 or 1550, was one of tremendous advance in other spheres, in political power, in wealth and in artistry. Those were the centuries when Gordon Childe's 'urban revolution' was completed; when the palace-complexes were built and decorated with astonishing frescoes; when the minor arts (vases and jewelry and seal-stones) reached their acme, with a style and spirit, a lightness and a delicate sense of movement, which are immediately recognized as Minoan and nothing else (*Plate IIa*); when society revealed itself in its visual arts as one that, at least at the top, had a psychology and style of life quite unlike any other of its day (or of any other age in antiquity for that matter).

Perhaps the most remarkable manifestation of Cretan originality was in the field of writing. When one considers how few systems of writing have ever been invented anywhere and at any time in world history, the Cretan contribution, within a relatively short period, seems beyond comprehension. First came a kind of modified picture-writing which Evans labelled 'hieroglyphic' on the analogy of the Egyptian script. There then emerged, in the early Middle Minoan centuries, a more sophisticated script, called 'Linear A' by Evans, in which most of the signs represented syllables. Linear A was widely dispersed on the island, the largest number of texts having so far been found at Haghia Triada and Kato Zakro. Eventually it gave way at Cnossus to Linear B, an outgrowth in a compli-cated way from Linear A.[1] Although Linear B, unlike Linear A, was also employed on the mainland of Greece, so far no examples have been found in Crete elsewhere than at Cnossus and quite recently at Chania.[2] The question remains open whether we are faced with an accident of ar-chaeology or with a phenomenon of Cretan history. If an attractive recent claim stands up that twenty-five 'stirrup-jars' with Linear B signs found in Thebes were manufac-tured in Chania, the balance of probability would swing towards the accidental explanation. The question is im-portant, for it is linked with such further issues as the extent and nature of Cnossian suzerainty in Crete, and the precise part which writing played in the society.[3]

Apart from signs engraved or scratched on pottery, seal-stones, libation-tables and various miscellaneous objects, Cretan writing is known to us in bulk only from small, leaf-shaped clay tablets totalling less than 4000, many of them mere fragments. Perishable materials, such as wax or papyrus, were no doubt also used, but no trace of them

[1] A few vases, clay lamps and other objects with from one to three Linear A signs have been found in Melos, Thera, Ceos and Naxos, but it is premature, to say the least, to draw any inferences about Cycladic 'lit-eracy' from such weak testimony. It is not unfair to point out that archaeologists have not always been able to distinguish mere scratches from Linear A signs.

[2] On Chania see E. Hallager in *Opuscula Atheniensia* 2 (1975) 53–86.

[3] Account must also be taken of yet another script, on a small disk from Phaestus, seemingly related to, but not identical with, the writing on a double axe found at Arkalochori in central Crete and to that on a limestone slab from Mallia, and of other bits and pieces. So far these iso-lated finds have produced a vast amount of commentary but no accept-able solutions.

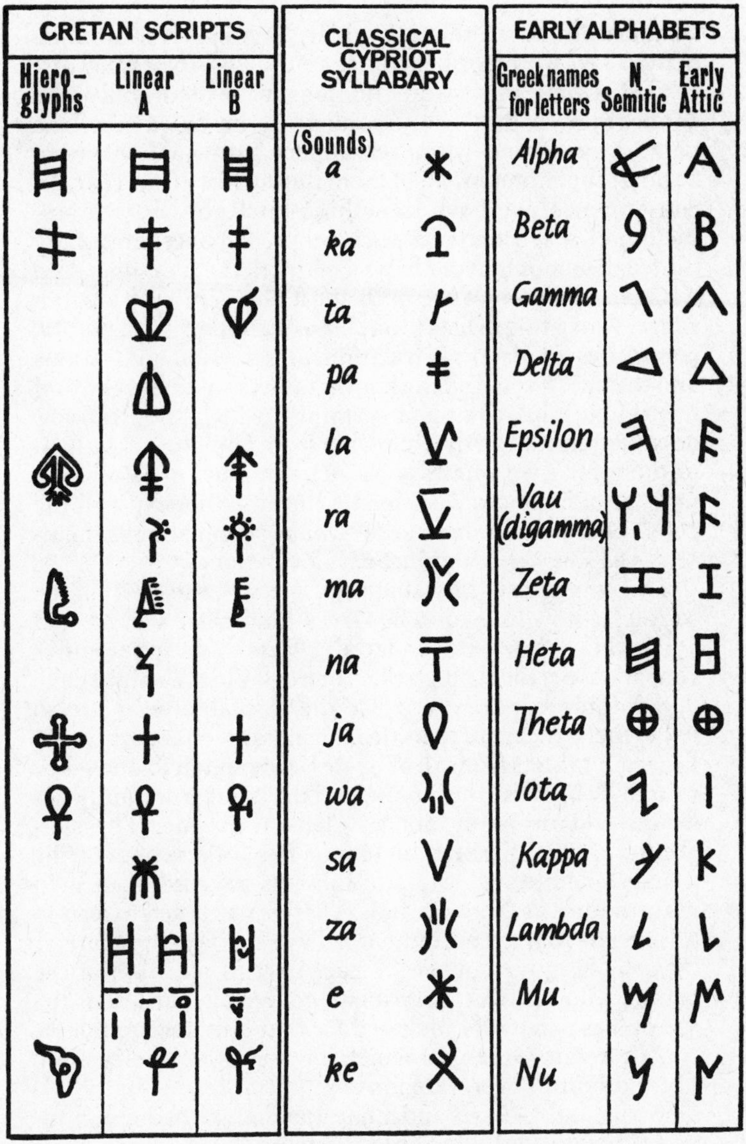

CRETAN SCRIPTS			CLASSICAL CYPRIOT SYLLABARY		EARLY ALPHABETS		
Hiero-glyphs	Linear A	Linear B			Greek names for letters	N. Semitic	Early Attic
目	目	目	(Sounds) a	✳	Alpha	⩤	A
✝	✝	✝	ka	⌓	Beta	9	B
	♛	♉	ta	⼁	Gamma	⼻	⋀
	⨁		pa	⧧	Delta	◁	△
♠	⬥	⬆	la	V	Epsilon	⧃	⪜
	⿃	⚙	ra	⩔	Vau (digamma)	Y, ⴘ	⪚
⬓	⬏	⬓	ma	ⵋ	Zeta	ⵑ	ⵕ
	⼋		na	⊤	Heta	ⵏ	⯄
✚	✝	✝	ja	◗	Theta	⊕	⊕
⚲	⚲	⚲	wa	ⵕⵍ	Iota	⟮		
	ⵋ		sa	⋁	Kappa	ⵤ	ⵖ
	目目	目	za	ⵕⵍⵍ	Lambda	⵨	⵨
	i i ⊖	⊤ i	e	✳	Mu	ⵯ	⵰
ⵕ	⵨	⵨	ke	✕	Nu	ⵈ	⵰

Figure 2 Scripts (none is complete)

remains. And even the clay tablets have survived by accident. They were not baked before use and they were discarded when they were no longer needed; only the conflagrations that accompanied the destruction of the palaces preserved whatever tablets happened to be on hand at the moment, all of them dating from that year. In consequence, we have something analogous to a cross-section of a cell under a microscope, lacking depth, any hint of development or change, of the element of time. And the texts themselves are both short and very restricted in range, consisting of lists of one kind or another, or of cryptic recordings of property relationships, ration allocations and the like. Even if all the known tablets could be read and translated with complete certainty, which they cannot, documents such as the following from Cnossus—'At Lasunthos (?): Two nurses, one girl, one boy' or 'Amnisos: One jar of honey to Eileithyia. One jar of honey to all the gods. One jar of honey ...'—would soon exhaust themselves as sources of significant information.

The language of the tablets in Linear B, the latest of the scripts, is now known to be Greek (and more will be said about this below). But so far all efforts to decipher either Linear A or the still earlier hieroglyphic writing have failed. This is partly because the available texts are so few—the Linear B texts from Cnossus outnumber the Linear A tablets from all of Crete by about ten to one—but primarily because the language of the latter is certainly not Greek and probably not any known tongue. The suggestion that it is a Semitic tongue has little support. The more plausible suggestion of Luwian, inferred from such place-names as Cnossus and Tylissus, has failed to lead to an even partial decipherment. All we can say, therefore, is that the language of the Linear A script was that of the people who created the Minoan golden age; and that the script was originally invented for that language and later transferred to Greek, for which it was not very well suited. Our ignorance even extends to important place-names. If Cnossus and Gortyn and Phaestus maintained a continued, though unimportant, existence, and hence their names, throughout ancient Greek history, other centres were destroyed and totally abandoned in the Bronze Age. Haghia Triada and Kato Zakro, for example, have had to be given identifying labels from contemporary landmarks: their own names are still unknown.

The tablets, in sum, have provided important supplementary information, some of it novel (especially on the history of the Greek language), but our basic source is still the material remains. Perhaps the most important contribution of the tablets is to reinforce the power implications inherent in the archaeology. Indeed, it can be argued that the needs of a centralized administration were a far greater impetus to the development of writing, among the Sumerians (cuneiform) as in Crete, than intellectual or spiritual needs. Between the Late Neolithic era and the Middle Minoan period there was a rapid increase in human and natural resources and a concentration, both socially and geographically, of the power to employ them. Otherwise the great palace-complexes could neither have been built nor have functioned. Only recently have two words turned up on a few tablets which apparently indicate the exchange of commodities. On the other hand, there are many inventories, ration-lists and lists of personnel. The implication is that the society was run from the palace-centre, which administered the internal economy in every detail, distributing people and goods, from raw materials to finished products, without the use of money or of a market mechanism. Some confirmation comes from a demonstration that the numerous Cnossus tablets listing sheep and wool—all of them, it must be remembered, dating in the year of the destruction of the site—record an annual census of flocks and shearings and of the shepherds responsible. The total number of animals was about 100,000, and, in so far as place-names can be identified, they seem to have been pastured all over central Crete. It therefore appears that the palace at Cnossus had some sort of sheep-and-wool monopoly in that sector of the island.

The suggestion then comes to mind that wool may help answer an old puzzle: how did the Cretans pay for (or otherwise obtain) the copper, gold, ivory and other things they had to import? Wool is now offered as at least part of the answer. And it is true that the Cretans (called Keftiu) represented on Egyptian frescoes sometimes carry folded cloths. But they also carried gold, silver, ivory and other things which are not Cretan products, so that this bit of concrete evidence for wool as a major trading commodity is somewhat weakened. At this point the tablets are frustratingly, and surprisingly, silent. They say nothing about the outside world in any respect: that world might just as well not have existed so far as the tablets are concerned. And archaeology alone, it cannot be repeated often enough, rarely can reveal the *mechanism* of foreign relations even when it unearths great quantities of foreign or foreign-inspired goods.

Another approach suggested by modern scholars is to put the stress on empire and tribute, on the so-called Minoan thalassocracy (rule of the sea), references to which are found in classical Greek writers. There can be no dispute either about the wealth and power of Cnossus or about Minoan seamanship. There seem to have been 'Minoan' settlements on some nearby islands, notably on Cythera to the north, where the peak was reached in Late Minoan I, not very long before the site was abandoned (with no trace of destruction). However, the further step to a wide-ranging maritime *empire*, in the usual sense of that word, is neither simple nor self-evident, and it can be argued that the whole notion is very weakly based. The first Greek mention of thalassocracy is by Herodotus and Thucydides in the second half of the fith century B.C., and that is far too late to be taken seriously by itself, without supporting evidence. The many Greek legends about prehistoric Crete have different emphases, mostly purely religious in character. The notable exception is the story of Theseus and the minotaur, which deserves special consideration.

The story runs like this. King Minos was married to Pasiphaë, daughter of the Sun, who developed an unnatural passion for a bull that had come out of the sea. She appealed to the divinely descended craftsman Daedalus, who constructed a contraption which enabled her to have intercourse with the beast. Pasiphaë then gave birth to a monster, half man, half bull, called the minotaur. On the king's orders, Daedalus built a labyrinth in which the monster was housed, and every year the Athenians, who were subjects of Minos, were required to supply seven youths and seven maidens to be fed to the minotaur. One year Theseus, the young son of the Athenian king, persuaded his father to include him in the annual consignment of victims. When Theseus arrived in Crete, he won the love of Minos' daughter Ariadne, and with her aid he slew the minotaur. The pair then fled to the island of Naxos; there Theseus deserted Ariadne, the god Dionysus found her and married her.

That tale, it has been claimed, reflects in mythical form Athenian subjection to, and then emancipation from, Cretan overlordship during the Bronze Age. But the objections to such an interpretation are grave. Although monsters of the half-man, half-animal type are common, particularly in Minoan seal-stones, only one or two harmless looking 'minotaurs' have been found. The bull, on the other hand, is amply documented as an important element in Minoan religion: as a sacrificial animal, or in the familiar 'bull-leaping' scenes, which are more likely to represent some form of ritual than a mere sport, or in small bronze statuettes found in some of the caves which were cult-centres. A possible explanation of the minotaur legend, therefore, is that it is a later tale devised to explain some ceremony, perhaps an initiation, linked with the worship of Dionysus, the original meaning of which had long been forgotten.[1] The alternative, that it is a concealed account of the overthrow of a foreign overlord, strains the imagination. History knows enough examples of traditional tales in which a people recounts how it once won

---

[1] This suggestion is buttressed by the persuasive arguments of Paul Faure, *Fonctions des cavernes crétoises* (*Travaux et mémoires* of the Ecole française d' Athènes XIV, 1964), pp. 166–73, that the labyrinth is to be identified not with the palace of Cnossus, but with a cave. He suggests the cave of Skotino, some miles east of Cnossus, where evidence of cult goes back to the beginning of the Middle Minoan period and persists into the Archaic Greek period. Religious continuity of such long duration is attested in not more than three or four Cretan caves.

independence, and they never disguise it so heavily as to conceal the fundamental point they are making. It may also be relevant that in the Middle Minoan period, Athens shows less trace of Cretan connexions, apart from artistic influences, than a number of other mainland centres.

Yet another puzzle is presented to us by the openness of the Cretan palaces, none of them citadels in the proper sense but unfortified 'civilian' complexes. The contrast with such mainland fortresses as Mycenae and Tiryns strikes every visitor. Minoan thalassocracy cannot be the explanation, often as it may be proposed. Threats from overseas have never been the only, or even the decisive, cause for fortification. They surely do not explain Mycenae or Tiryns any more than a medieval castle. Was there never any danger of conflict between palaces? Was there no need for compulsion and police protection at home? Yet everywhere one turns in Crete, peacefulness is the prevailing tone. The caves, which became havens of refuge in troubled times throughout Cretan history, ancient and modern, were uninhabited during the palace-era. Arms, armour and chariots are recorded in the Linear B tablets from Cnossus, but they are remarkably rare in the figured monuments of any nature or size. They are even rare in the graves; it is only after the occupation by Greek-speaking people from the mainland that one can properly talk of warrior-graves at all.

Whatever the explanation of this phenomenon, it is one reason for stressing the uniqueness of Crete. The palace-centred society and its obsessively detailed records are reminiscent of Ugarit in North Syria or Mari on the Euphrates. But, as has already been said, the psychology and the values at the top were radically different in many respects, whatever may have been the case with the mass of the population, about whom we know nothing. Although not a line of writing exists, either from Crete or from the much more abundant documentation of her neighbours, near or far, which tells us anything explicit of the thinking of Bronze Age Crete, of their *ideas* on any subject, it is possible to draw some inferences from the material remains about their differences from the other centralized societies of their day.

Babylonian, Egyptian and Hittite rulers filled their lands with monumental evidence of their power, and of the power of their gods. Cretan rulers did nothing of the kind, neither in their palaces nor in their tombs. There is nothing majestic or central about the throne-room at Cnossus, whether in its size or in its wall-decoration (with its mythical animals and floral designs, but without a single portrait). Even the throne is not particularly regal. Not a single picture exists which portrays an historical event or which reveals administrative or judicial activity or any other manifestation of political power in action.

As for the gods and goddesses, they are difficult to discover at all. They seem to have been fairly numerous, but they were not housed in temples and so there was no need for the cult-statue characteristic of both contemporary Near Eastern and later Greek civilizations. Worship was carried on in small domestic shrines, in sacred places out of doors, and in about twenty-five of the caves in various parts of the island (by and large, not the more spectacular caves, and not all of them in use simultaneously). In the ceremonies, the stress was on an epiphany, on the temporary appearance of a divinity in response to prayer, to sacrifice, or—most characteristically and originally Cretan—to ritual dancing. In many of the scenes, it is the ecstasy of the worshippers which is central rather than the god in person; indeed, the act of anticipation alone is sometimes portrayed without the actual epiphany. The site of the epiphany was a sacred tree, a pillar, occasionally an architectural façade. Given this stress on the worshippers, on the human side of the relationship, it was appropriate that, except for a few frescoes and an occasional sarcophagus, these scenes should have been engraved on rings, sealstones and small ceramic objects. Otherwise, the evidence for religion consists largely of such symbolic objects as the double axe and the 'horns of consecration',[1] the interpretation of which remains much disputed; of the equipment used in libations and sacrifices; especially in the caves, of the ashes and bones of sacrificial victims, bulls, sheep,

[1] There were no obvious solar or astral symbols, it is worth noting.

pigs, dogs and other animals;[1] and of objects dedicated to
the gods, including pottery, swords and shields, a variety
of feminine articles, animal statuettes, and, eventually,
human figurines, which were revived in Middle Minoan
Crete after a long hiatus. Usually it is impossible to distinguish human from divine figures, except by the most
subjective canons. If a few, such as the so-called snake
goddess, are accurately attributed, they are anyway a late
innovation, probably under eastern influence. And even
then the traditional smallness of scale was strictly preserved.

This lack of monumentality is a fitting accompaniment
to the absence of the external manifestations of war, to the
specific qualities and the tone of Cretan works of art. Even
the large frescoes are not effectively monumental (outside
of Cnossus they are uncommon and almost entirely devoid
of human figures). They have a lightness and mobility
which are original and rare, if not unique, in the Bronze
Age anywhere, qualities which are created with magnifi-
cent technical skill on the vases, gems and small bronzes
(notably in the latter case those from Tylissus). But they
tend, with their highly stylized subject-matter and treatment of such details as dress and posture, to a monotonous
conventionality, a preciousness and prettiness inappro-
priate to their size. Life is all games and ritual, but one sees
little human passion, personal joy or suffering. Life has a
tinkly quality, they seem to say, without depth. Hence the
minor arts are the greatest Cretan triumph after the bour-
geois comforts of good drainage and sanitation, lighting
and airiness in the palaces.

The impression, admittedly speculative, is that early in
the Middle Minoan period Cretan society became institu-
tionally and ideologically fixed, that it found an equilibrium which was not seriously challenged for centuries,
which was safe in all directions, perhaps too passively safe.
Thereafter a further refinement in skills, expansion of

[1] The complete skeleton of a bull has been found in a tomb, dated by
the excavators soon after 1400 B.C., at Arkhanes, about six miles from
Cnossus; see *Illustrated London News* for 26 March, 1966, pp. 32–3. This is
the first example of a bull-sacrifice from a tomb.

population, further additions to the palaces can still be seen, but it was mostly on a horizontal line, so to speak. That is why it is possible to picture this world without any reference at all to shifts from Middle to Late Minoan. Although that particular break is archaeologically valid, chiefly in the pottery, the style of life seems to have been little altered. Many parts of Crete were severely damaged by earthquake in the Middle Minoan III period, but the catastrophe was followed not only by immediate rebuilding, but by further growth, by the creation of new settlements, and by much closer contacts with the Greek mainland. But not by anything pointing to significant social or psychological innovations.

Then there came a time when, somehow, men from mainland Greece took control in Cnossus, and, through the power of Cnossus, of much of central Crete. The decisive proof is the fact that the language of the Linear B tablets from Cnossus is Greek (and indistinguishable from the Greek of the mainland tablets). Unfortunately, as has already been said, all the tablets date from the moment of destruction, so that they offer no clue as to the date of Greek penetration. All the indicators, however, suggest that this occurred at the beginning of the Cnossian stage, Late Minoan II (a century or so after the beginning of Late Helladic on the mainland), when there was a qualitative change in the tombs, among other things, following mainland models and including genuine warrior-graves for the first time in Crete. At about the same time, such centres as Phaestus and Mallia ceased to be 'royal residences', and the great palace at Kato Zakro on the eastern tip of the island, the fourth largest in Crete, was totally abandoned after a natural disaster (and it was not re-discovered until 1961).[1] The implication appears to be that the new rulers of Cnossus acquired some sort of suzerainty over a sizeable

[1] Persistent efforts have been made to attribute the Cretan phenomena to wind-blown ash and tidal waves produced by a massive volcanic eruption at Santorini. The causal link is untenable, above all (but not only) because the Santorini eruption occurred half a century too early (1500 B.C.); see the brief report by M. Popham in *Antiquity* 53 (1979) 57–60. The *permanent* abandonment of Kato Zakro must have had a social or political cause.

portion of the island, without themselves moving in large numbers to other centres. That would explain why Late Minoan II is not discoverable as an 'independent' stage outside Cnossus.

Late Minoan II saw Cnossus at the height of its power. Ever since Evans, the end of that period has been dated to about 1400 B.C. (or perhaps three decades later on the current view). It was thus a relatively brief era, ending in catastrophe. Earthquake may have been a factor but it cannot be a sufficient explanation, because this time, unlike previous occasions, there was no recovery. Life went on in Crete, but the age of power and palaces was over forever. Henceforth the mainland was to occupy the centre of the stage. Perhaps a natural disaster, if that is really what happened, was followed by an expulsion from Crete of the Greek overlords through some sort of popular uprising, which also swept away the remnants of native power that the Greek intruders had seriously weakened a century or so earlier. But these are speculations for which no firm foundation exists. They would be undermined, it should be added, if recent suggestions could be substantiated that the fall of Cnossus is to be brought down to 1200 or even 1150 B.C., to coincide with the end of the mainland Bronze Age civilization. But the evidence, accepted by the preponderance of expert opinion, supports the traditional dating.[1]

[1] See M. R. Popham, *The Destruction of the Palace at Knossos* (Göteborg: Paul Aström, 1970).

5

Mycenaean Civilization

AT a date which falls within the great Cretan palace-period, that is, towards the end of Middle Minoan III, about 1600 B.C., something happened on the Greek mainland which gave a radically new turn to developments there, and to the history of the Aegean generally. Precisely what happened remains mysterious, the subject of continuing speculation and controversy without agreement, but the visible consequences are clear enough. Mycenae suddenly became a centre of wealth and power, and of a warrior civilization, without an equal in this region. Soon other important centres arose in central and southern Greece, and influences then radiated to the Aegean islands and the coasts of Asia Minor and Syria in the east, and to Sicily and southern Italy in the west. The next four hundred years or so, both on the mainland and in many of the islands, reveal such uniformity in the archaeological record that, by an unfortunate convention, the label 'Mycenaean' has come to be applied to the whole civilization (though it was never used in antiquity). There is no harm done if the label is retained in an abstract sense, comparable to 'Islamic', but the danger must be avoided of sliding over to an implication of centralized political authority, of a territorially extensive society ruled from Mycenae, as the Assyrian Empire, for example, was ruled from Assur. There is, as we shall see, no justification for such a political implication.

The remarkable prelude to this civilization is fully attested only at Mycenae. It amounts to no more than two grave circles, an older one the pivotal date of which is 1600 B.C., excavated by Greek archaeologists late in 1951, now known as Circle B, and another perhaps a century later (Circle A), which Heinrich Schliemann found in 1876 (six years after his discovery of Troy) to make the fundamental breakthrough in modern study of the Greek Bronze Age.

Figure 3 Grave stele from Circle B, Mycenae

Both circles were part of a large cemetery, presumably outside the settlement proper. Three features are noteworthy: first, the circles were deliberately marked out and were intended to be significant; second, the grave goods were numerous, luxurious and in part warlike; and third, the idea of memorializing power and authority was wholly concentrated in these tombs, for no trace of the settlement has been found, which must mean that there were neither walls nor fortifications nor palaces built of stone. The actual burials were scattered irregularly within the circles, in ordinary graves or cists or deep burial shafts—some twenty-four in Circle B, only six in Circle A, all the latter of the deep shaft type.

The interments themselves were no radical departure from older practices, nor was the unceremonious pushing aside of earlier bones and grave-goods to make room for later corpses. But everything else was new. The graves were marked on the surface by upright stone slabs (Figure 3), many of them inscribed with figured decorations or animals or military and hunting scenes (but never with a name or a proper portrait or other immediate link with a particular personality, thus remaining strictly within the Bronze Age tradition of the anonymity of power). The circle must have had some sacral significance, which survived a long time. In the great building programme on the citadel after 1300 B.C., when the 1000-yard circuit wall was constructed, Circle A was brought within the precinct and retained as 'hallowed' ground, marked off by an elaborate double ring of limestone slabs. Whatever the builders of that period may have known or believed about the grave circle, the impulse behind their beliefs was a powerful one, since by that time the original surface was well underground and they would have given themselves far less trouble had they ignored it.

It would require pages to give an adequate account of the contents of the richest of the graves, numbers III, IV and V of Circle A. Karo's catalogue of grave III alone includes 183 numbered items, and that figure is an understatement, since many of the 'items' include more than one object, in one instance 'sixty-four small circular gold disks [engraved] with butterflies[1] (*Plate II b*). All the traditional luxury materials were employed, gold above all, the latter in a quantity and workmanship for which the only surviving parallels are among the Scythian burial finds in southern Russia and the royal Macedonian tombs in Vergina, a thousand and more years later. Alongside much delicate, even feminine, gold-leaf and filigree work in ornaments of all kinds, there were masses of swords and other possessions of the warrior. What is missing is anything like the Cycladic 'idols', anything that is not obviously utilitarian in an earthly sense (weapons, utensils and ornaments). Both in the materials employed and in the artistic skills and styles, there are reminiscences of, and borrowings from, the civilizations outside. Yet fundamentally the whole is original in workmanship and style, a new creation of the rulers at Mycenae and their craftsmen.

Whoever the men and women were who were buried in these specially prepared graves, they were at the top of a power structure within the community different from any Greece had known before. It is tempting to link their emergence with the arrival of the battle chariot and the long sword, though the first graves in Circle B seem a bit early for that. In any event, chariots figure prominently on the slabs marking the later shaft-graves, as in the still later Linear B inventories from Cnossus and Pylos. The chariot was an import—the idea, that is, not the actual vehicles themselves—but that is no argument that the people who took advantage of this new military weapon were themselves migrants. Nor is the abundant gold, which might represent the fruits of mercenary service, for example in Egypt as some scholars believe, or of successful raiding, or of trade, or of all three in combination. For the present we must confess that the causes of the sudden upsurge in power and the possession of treasure are unknown.

The shaft-graves and their contents reveal a steady increase in technical and artistic skills and in concentration of power. Similar growth occurred in many parts of central Greece and the Peloponnese during Late Helladic I

[1] G. Karo, *Die Schachtgräber von Mykenai* (2 vols., Munich, 1930–3), I, p. 43.

and II (subdivisions which are hard to distinguish anyway), but outside Mycenae (and eventually in Mycenae too) the visible symbol was a very different kind of burial-chamber, the spectacular *tholos-* or bee-hive-tomb. These were circular chambers cut into the hillside, with a special runway (*dromos*) leading to them, roofed over by the careful building up of a dome-like frame of stones in ever-decreasing rings, ending with a capstone above the natural height of the hill. The whole structure was sealed and covered with earth, leaving an imposing mound in view. Some idea of the scale can be had from the dimensions of the greatest and one of the latest of them all, the popularly but inaccurately named 'Treasury of Atreus' at Mycenae (*Plate III*): 48 feet in diameter, 43 feet in height (both inside measurements), a *dromos* 118 feet in length, and a lintel over the entrance-door weighing perhaps 100 tons.

Nothing prepares us for such tombs. There is no architectural forerunner, either in Greece or anywhere else. But any doubt that they indicate not just power but more or less unique status in the hierarchy, kingship in effect, is removed by the co-existence with the *tholos*-tombs of many chamber-tombs containing rich grave-goods, the resting-places of families well up the hierarchical scale but not at the top. The spread and location of the new dynasties in central and southern Greece can be plotted on a map by following the erection of *tholos*-tombs, the largest number of which were constructed in the fifteenth century (Late Helladic II). The word 'dynastic' is justified by the evidence of successive burials over several generations (in the chamber-tombs as well), each requiring considerable effort to re-open and re-seal the chamber. It should be added that there is no way of telling whether the dynasties remained within single families or not: usurpers are not distinguishable in their graves.

The *tholos*-tomb period is also the age when mainland activity becomes clearly visible abroad, in the form of extensive pottery finds, at first primarily in the west (Sicily and southern Italy), but by the end of Late Helladic II also in the other direction, in Rhodes, in Cyprus, in Miletus, in

Asia Minor, and elsewhere, an activity which mounted to a crescendo in the final phase of the Bronze Age, in Late Helladic III A and B. It is at this point that the limitations of the Linear B tablets are particularly exasperating. They have been found in considerable numbers in Pylos (and a few in Mycenae, Tiryns and Thebes), and thus far nowhere else on the mainland. They are comparable in language and content to those from Cnossus, equally lacking in the dimension of time because they, too, date from a moment of destruction and conflagration. If the commonly accepted date (soon after 1400) for the fall of Cnossus is right, then Greek speakers took control there at the height of the *tholos*-tomb period. But we do not know where in Greece they came from. It is a gratuitous assumption to suggest that they were from Mycenae itself. Nor do we know when and where on the mainland writing first made its appearance, in the Linear B script. To make matters worse, mass-produced 'Mycenaean' pottery before the III C period tended to be sufficiently uniform in style and technique to render it difficult and often impossible to distinguish among places of manufacture.[1] When, therefore, a modern writer refers to 'Mycenaean pottery' found, for example, in the Lipari Islands, he means pottery from somewhere in the Mycenaean world, which eventually included such places as Rhodes and Cyprus, and not necessarily from mainland Greece, let alone from Mycenae itself. (Often, indeed, it was probably a local 'imitation'.)

The question of the relations between the mainland centres and those sites in which pottery finds are particularly concentrated is therefore a most troublesome one. That there was extensive trade (and that the mainland was beginning to compete with Crete by the end of the third millennium) can be taken as certain. Some materials, such as amber and ivory, could not have been brought to Greece otherwise, nor, in all probability, could most of the gold, tin and copper. Scattered Mycenaean objects and motifs reached central Europe, from about 1500 B.C., and their

---

[1] Perhaps scientific analysis of the clays will eventually make distinctions possible, but that study is still in its infancy.

III Interior of the largest *tholos*-tomb, popularly known as the Treasury of Atreus, Mycenae

IV Bronze tripod and cauldron, 61 cm high, ninth century B.C., found in Olympia

presence is to be explained by the Mycenaean need for metals. Amber is common in Greece from the shaft-graves to the end of the Mycenaean age, though rare in Minoan Crete and post-Mycenaean Greece, and much of it is Baltic in origin.[1]

But who were the traders and under what conditions did they operate? The Linear B tablets from the mainland are as silent on these questions as are those from Cnossus. Very likely the concentration of Mycenaean pottery at Scoglio del Tonno in the Taranto region of southern Italy reveals the presence of a 'Mycenaean' trading post, linked with the movement of goods from central and western Europe. It is not so easy, however, to find satisfactory criteria for assessing the view of some writers that Rhodes and Miletus were Mycenaean colonies. That the material remains in those two places (unlike Cyprus) look 'Mycenaean' is true, but that proves nothing about their *political* connexions with the mainland, one way or the other. If we had no more information than that about classical Rhodes and Miletus in the year 400 B.C., we might guess them to be colonies by the same reasoning, and we should of course be wrong. The decipherment of Linear B has thrown new light on the relations between the mainland and Cnossus; yet even now it is not certain whether the take-over of Cnossus by Greek speakers was followed by actual allegiance or subjection to a mainland power. Trade, migration, conquest and colonialism do not always interact in a neat package.

Nor are the political relations clear on the mainland itself. The notable fact has already been mentioned that the *tholos*-tombs are earlier than large-scale domestic architecture, that, in other words, the kings and nobles lavished their wealth and expressed their power, architecturally, in their burial-chambers before they turned their attention to their palaces and houses. The excavators at Pylos have found evidence of an extensive settlement of the lower town earlier than the construction of the great palace, but they cannot trace its history back very far, and

---

[1] This has been determined by infra-red absorption spectrophotometry; see the series of articles by C. W. Beck and others in *Greek, Roman and Byzantine Studies*, the most recent in vol. 13 (1972), pp. 359–85.

that is the picture in Greece generally. We know that the population had grown considerably and that they were clustered in villages, usually on hillsides overlooking the farmland. (Nearly 500 Mycenaean settlements on the mainland have already been located.) And we know that society had become hierarchically stratified, ruled by a warrior class under chieftains or kings. Then, after 1400 (and in most places not until about 1300) there came the dramatic shift from concentration on impressive burial-chambers to the erection of a number of palace-fortresses. Such places as Tiryns and Mycenae in the eastern Peloponnese, the Acropolis in Athens, Thebes and Gla in Boeotia, now looked more like medieval fortress-towns than like the open, agglutinative Cretan complexes. There was still cell-like growth, but the nucleus was the so-called *megaron* type of house, consisting of a columned fore-porch or vestibule, a long main room and usually a store-room behind.

This stress on fortification and the warlike cannot have been merely a matter of taste. Something in the social situation required it, as presumably it was not needed, at least not on anything like such a scale, in Crete. The mainland Linear B tablets record the same activities and the same kinds of inventories as at Cnossus, the same pattern of palace control and administration over the community and over the surrounding region (but not at any considerable distance beyond). However, the tablets give no clues about the warlike factor, for which we must try to draw implications from the distribution and fate of the fortresses themselves. In simplified form, the key question may be posed like this. Why were the Argolid and the region around Corinth relatively thick with fortresses, whereas in Messenia to the west, Pylos was only lightly fortified and a day's march to the north there were large *tholos*-tombs and a heavily fortified hilltop site at Peristeria, the ancient name for which is unknown? There was a considerable settlement at Argos in the Middle Helladic period, and then again continuously from Late Helladic II on, but there was no palace, no fortification, not a single *tholos*-tomb, no arms in the graves. Apparently Argos was subject to Mycenae six miles to the north, or to the slightly less distant Tiryns in the south, and had no warrior aristocracy of its own. On the other hand, it is hard to imagine that Mycenae and Tiryns were on a par, dividing the Argive plain between them (or that Thebes and Gla were equal powers in Boeotia). In the generations following the early *tholos*-tombs, persistent raids and wars presumably raised a few successful dynasts to positions of super-power and suzerainty, with the lesser or defeated chieftains destroyed in some instances, and in others allowed to survive in some form of subordinate status. There are signs at several places, for example, Mycenae, Tiryns and Thebes, of heavy destruction and burning in this period, followed by changes in the building-complex and the fortifications. That suggests war damage. No doubt there were also inter-dynastic marriages to complicate the succession to the throne and the inter-state relations, as they always do.

The picture that emerges from such an analysis of the tablets and the archaeology combined is one of a division of Mycenaean Greece into a number of petty bureaucratic states, with a warrior aristocracy, a high level of craftsmanship, extensive foreign trade in necessities (metals) and luxuries, and a permanent condition of armed neutrality at best in their relations with each other, and perhaps at times with their subjects. Nothing points to an over-all authority on the part of Mycenae. That notion rests wholly on the Homeric poems, in which Agamemnon is commander-in-chief of a coalition army on an expedition against Troy (and in which his authority is easily flouted, it should be noted). But the contemporary evidence argues that, whatever the authority of the ruler of Mycenae over the Argolid may have been, Pylos owed him nothing, nor Thebes or Iolkos.[1]

Apart from some battle scenes, Mycenaean palace art fails to reflect in any direct way the warrior-society. That art is, indeed, astonishingly derivative (except in pottery), with the same love of abstract and floral decoration, the

[1] The difficult problem of the worth of the Homeric poems as evidence for the Mycenaean civilization is discussed briefly in Chapter 6 and more fully in Chapter 7.

same monotonous processionals, the same conventionality and static quality as its Cretan prototypes. There is the same impersonality, too. Almost never, for example, is a 'foreigner' portrayed, distinguishable in features, dress, hair or beard. Nor was the monumentality of the architecture transferred to painting or sculpture, a fact which becomes all the more striking when one remembers that by the thirteenth century there had been close contact with both Anatolia and Egypt. There is not even anything comparable in scale to the Middle Helladic life-sized statues from Ceos (mentioned in Chapter 3).

Although the Linear B tablets abound with names of gods and goddesses, and with lists of what appear to be personnel in their service or of offerings to them, Mycenaean religion is archaeologically still less noticeable than Minoan. There are altars and there are representations of divinities and rituals on gems and seal-stones, most of them Cretan in origin without any distinguishing features to mark them off as Mycenaean, but, until the summer of 1968, no clearly identifiable shrine or special room for ritual purposes had been found within the palace-complexes. That summer and the next a building was excavated at Mycenae, dating from the final decades before the destruction of the site, consisting of a large room in which there were platforms so arranged, with associated objects, as to indicate cult activity. Adjoining was a small sealed 'store-room' (about six feet square) in which were stacked, among other things, some sixteen hollow nude figures in clay, four male, five female, another probably female, and two hermaphrodite, up to two feet in height, with short upraised or extended arms (but no legs), notional breasts, hair and facial features added afterwards as was done with handles and spouts on vases. The room also contained six coiled clay snakes, realistically modelled. The latter are rather splendid objects (Plate IIc), but the statuettes are extremely 'primitive' and ugly, save for a single exceptional small one, which is clothed and painted.[1]

In every significant respect this find is unique so far.

[1] See Lord William Taylour in *Antiquity* 43 (1969) 91–7; 44 (1970) 270–80.

Snakes are common in association with human figures, but these are the first known from anywhere in the Aegean in the Bronze Age to be portrayed independently. The statues are unlike any others in their over-all appearance (though similarities in technique of manufacture and in their posture have been suggested with one group of Cretan figures). And no other such 'store-room' has been found. All of which serves as a warning that most general statements about Mycenaean culture are tentative in the nature of the case. One is almost reluctant to record the fact that, at present, only at Eleusis, Ceos, Delos and possibly Melos have reasonably certain traces been discovered of other 'temples' in the Mycenaean era; or to comment that it is perhaps not accidental that none of these places was a centre of secular power.

6

The End of the Bronze Age

IN the surviving Hittite archives there are about twenty
texts of the third quarter of the second millennium that
refer to a 'kingdom' of Achchiyawa. It appears to have
been more or less independent, on the western rim of
Hittite territory, and to have been a source of trouble,
especially towards the end when the Hittite Empire was
beginning to lose its grip. Ever since these documents were
deciphered more than a generation ago, there have been
attempts to equate the people of Achchiyawa with the
Achaeans, the most common of the names in the Homeric
poems for the Greeks in the Trojan War, and, therefore,
presumably the name (or a name) by which they knew
themselves in what we have come to call the Mycenaean
age. The arguments are technical, complicated and not
finally conclusive, but the equation has been rendered
increasingly untenable by linguistic analysis, continued
archaeological discovery and a reconsideration of the once
accepted Hittite royal chronology.[1] At most, we are left
with nothing more significant than the possibility that
some 'Mycenaean Greeks' from the coast of Asia Minor or
the offshore islands shared in the chronic buccaneering
and warring on the edges of the Hittite sphere of influence.

The Hittite Empire was actually broken up by 1200 or
1190. Although we have no direct textual evidence from
which to identify the people who accomplished that, there
is a growing probability that there was some sort of link
with the considerable incursions into the eastern Aegean
by a loose coalition of peoples twice mentioned in Egyptian
sources, from a careless reading of which they have
acquired the misleading name of the 'Sea Peoples'. The
first reference is to an attack on the Nile Delta by Libyans
and their mercenaries—'northerners coming from all

[1] See G. Steiner in *Saeculum* 15 (1964) 365–92; J. D. Muhly in *Historia*
23 (1974) 129–45; A Kammenhuber in *Orientalia* 39 (1970) 278–301.

lands'—in the reign of the pharaoh Merneptah, about 1220, who were thrown back, the Egyptians claimed, with losses in killed and captured running into five figures. Among the mercenaries were the Akawash (or Ekwesh[1]), whom some have been tempted to identify with the Achaeans, from the name, despite the fact that the text makes a particular point of their being circumcised, a practice foreign to the Greeks of historical times and not attested for Bronze Age Greece either.

The second reference is far more serious. At the beginning of the twelfth century (perhaps as early as 1191), Ramses III stopped a full-scale invasion of the 'Sea Peoples' who were descending on Egypt by land and sea from Syria. 'No land could stand before their arms from Hatti, Kode, Carchemish, Arzawa and Alasiya on.'[2] Pharaonic triumphal claims are wildly unreliable, but there is every reason to accept the hard core of this boastful account, that the Egyptians had thrown back a combined tribal migration and invasion reminiscent of the later Germanic movements into the Roman Empire, scything through extensive territory before being defeated or coming to rest. The Akawash are not mentioned this time, and, because of the complications, already noted with foreign names written in hieroglyphics, there is no scholarly agreement about the identification of the various peoples save one, the Peleset, or Philistines, who after the defeat settled on the Palestinian coast, and gave that region the name it still bears.

Philistine sites are filled, almost from the moment of settlement, with Mycenaean III C pottery manufactured locally, whereas they have no III B. The importance of this is that the shift from III B to III C is everywhere—on the Greek mainland, in the islands, and also at Troy—the line which marks the end of the last great phase of the Bronze Age. That end was more abrupt than most breakdowns of

---

[1] One difficulty in identifying names in Egyptian hieroglyphic texts is that only the consonants are given, not vowels.

[2] Translated by J. A. Wilson in *Ancient Near Eastern Texts relating to the Old Testament*, ed. J. B. Pritchard (2 ed., Princeton University Press, 1955), p. 262.

past civilizations. From Thessaly in the north to Laconia and Messenia in the south, at least a dozen fortresses and palace-complexes were smashed, including Iolkos, Crisa (near Delphi), Gla, Pylos, Mycenae, and the one in the region of Sparta lying beneath the ruins of classical times. Other fortified settlements, and even cemeteries, were abandoned. Archaeologically all this destruction must be dated in the same period about 1200, and it is hard to imagine that it bore no connexion whatever with the activity of the 'Sea Peoples' and the destroyers of the Hittite Empire. The coincidence would be too remarkable, all the more so when the further fact is taken into account that there was turbulence as far east as Mesopotamia, and in the west, too, in Italy, the Lipari Islands and Sicily, perhaps even in France and north to the Baltic Sea. A large-scale movement of people is indicated, and there is a growing conviction among experts, based on archaeology and on inferences drawn from the further spread of Indo-European languages, that the original centre of disturbance was in the Carpatho-Danubian region of Europe. The 'movement' was neither organized nor concerted in the way a genuine coalition is. It appears rather to have been broken in rhythm, pushing in different directions at different times, as in the case of Egypt, attacked once from the west and a second time, a generation or so later, from the northeast. There was little stability in the inter-relationships among the migrants, uncertainty in the ultimate objectives. All that is analogous with the later Germanic movements, as is the fact that trading and cultural interchanges and influences, at least with Greece, had been going on for centuries before the raids began.

In so far as the people of Greece were concerned, the attack came against them from the immediate north, wherever the ultimate beginnings may have been. It was perhaps in this context that a massive wall was begun across the Isthmus of Corinth, traces of which are still preserved at the southeastern end. If so, it was of no avail. The intruders penetrated successfully and destroyed the fortresses of the Peloponnese, and with them the political organization and the settlement pattern they had been designed to protect.[1] Before the effects can be examined, however, it is necessary to consider a further complication, the story of Troy in the northwestern corner of Asia Minor.

The citadel of Troy, situated on a ridge a few miles from the Aegean Sea and the Dardanelles, overlooking and controlling a fertile plain, had no known Neolithic phase. It was first occupied at the beginning of the Bronze Age, about 3000 B.C., and was a fortress from the start. Throughout its long Early Bronze Age phase, down to the beginning of the second millennium, Trojan archaeology reveals a remarkable continuity of culture. Not that the centuries were altogether peaceful: there were periodic catastrophes, hence the division into five clearly marked stages, but each break seems to have been followed by immediate reconstruction without any visible indications of a new element in the population. Troy II was the richest of the five, showing rather impressive gold-work (the first 'treasure' found by Schliemann) several centuries before the shaft-graves of Mycenae. What followed was poorer, not to say mean, but apparently without a break in the continuity. Archaeologically Troy's early culture is linked with contemporary finds in the northern Aegean islands and the Cyclades, in Thrace and Macedonia, and, curiously, far west in the Lipari Islands—but not at all with the Hittites or Syria (though further excavations in northwestern Asia Minor may yet produce parallels closer to home). No other clues are available since not one scrap of writing has been found at Troy, nor is there a clear reference to the place in contemporary records elsewhere.

Then early in the second millennium came Troy VI, a new civilization that appeared without warning, as was the case with some of the important innovations elsewhere in the Aegean. It became much the most powerful of all the phases of Troy, culminating in a period of advanced technology, with complex fortification-walls, but lacking either treasure or aesthetically interesting work in any other field. The ruins contain horse bones, and it was

[1] The once standard view that the Dorians were the intruders who destroyed the Mycenaean world has nothing to support it.

apparently the horse that gave the new occupants a considerable, perhaps decisive, advantage over their predecessors. The quantities of Minyan ware and later of imported Mycenaean III A pottery indicate close connexions with Greece. After about 500 years, Troy VI was destroyed by a catastrophe so tremendous that earthquake is indicated rather than human causes. The immediate reoccupation, Troy VIIa, reveals no cultural changes, but, as after Troy II, a very reduced scale and standard in all respects. And it is this shrunken city which coincides with the last great phase in Greece, Mycenaean III B beginning about 1300. The date of *its* fall is then tied up with all the problems of the end of the Mycenaean world we are considering.

Troy VIIa was destroyed by man; that is clear from the archaeology. The date can be determined only by the pottery finds, and specifically by the fact that VIIa had only Mycenaean III B pottery, whereas III C turned up in the short-lived VIIb period (though unfortunately the finds are not sufficient to permit an answer to the question of how early in VIIb the new style made its first appearance[1]). Other things being equal, the conclusion would be drawn, at least tentatively, that the fall of Troy VIIa was part of the general cataclysm of about 1200 throughout the Aegean area. But other things are not equal because of the Greek tradition of the Trojan War, of a great coalition from the mainland that invaded and sacked Troy. If that tradition has any historical kernel in it, the Trojan War could have occurred, from the Greek side, only in the III B period, and therefore as a war against Troy VIIa. That the ruins are too paltry for Homer's great city of Priam is not a serious objection; so much exaggeration must be allowed any drawn out oral tradition. However, the date is a crux. Obviously no organized Mycenaean invasion of Troy was possible as late as 1200, for the Greek powers were themselves under attack or already smashed by then. To move the war back a generation would get

[1] Nor, unfortunately, is it possible to fix precisely enough the appearance in Troy VIIb of 'knobbed ware', a kind of pottery which seems to have had a central European origin.

round this difficulty, but to do that creates complications in correlating the dates of the finds at Troy with those from the major Greek sites. A small minority of scholars therefore propose abandoning the Greek tradition as essentially mythical, and removing Troy from its unique place in late Greek Bronze Age history, or indeed from any significant place in that history at all.

Whatever the truth about the fall of Troy, there is no dispute about the magnitude of the catastrophe in Greece. However, to speak bluntly of the end or destruction of a civilization is to involve oneself in ambiguities unless the notion is analysed and its aspects specified. Destruction meant in the first instance the smashing of palaces and their fortress-complexes. With them, we have the right to assume, went the particular pyramidal social structure out of which they had been created in the first place. Thus, the *tholos*-tomb disappeared, with a few rather mysterious and out of the way exceptions in Thessaly and perhaps in Messenia. The cist-grave now became the rule again, as it presumably had been for the lower classes during the Mycenaean period. The art of writing also disappeared. That may seem incredible, until the point is grasped that the sole function of writing in the Mycenaean world known to us on the available evidence was to meet the administrative needs of the palace. When the latter disappeared, the need and the art both went with it. And the palace disappeared so completely that it never again returned in the subsequent history of ancient Greece. Places like Mycenae, Tiryns and Iolkos were still inhibited in the III C period, after 1200, but the palaces were not reconstituted, and no Linear B tablets from this period have been found in Mycenae or anywhere else.

So basic a change, initiated by an invading population, necessarily altered the general settlement pattern. Not only was there an over-all decline in population at the end of III B, very sharp in some regions, but there were shifts and movements which went on for a long time. Some large centres were totally abandoned, for example Pylos and Gla. Others, such as Athens and Thebes, continued in occupation on a somewhat reduced scale. Still other

Figure 4 Pottery styles

a Mycenaean IIIB (10 cm high, from Attica)

b Mycenaean IIIB (15 cm high, found in late Troy VI)

c Mycenaean IIIC (10 cm high, from Athens)

d Protogeometric (15 cm high, from Athens)

e

e Geometric (77 cm high, from Thera)

areas—eastern Attica, the coast of Euboea nearest the mainland, Asine on the Argive coast, the district of Achaea on the gulf of Corinth (of which Patras is the modern centre), the island of Cephallenia in the Ionian Sea—now held larger populations than before. Some of this irregularity in the pattern no doubt resulted from further conflicts and expulsions that must have followed after the main initial shock, evidenced by still further damage at Mycenae and Tiryns about 1150. And there is reason to believe that smaller, subordinate communities—Argos, for example—received different treatment from the main centres of power.

In such difficult and confused times, one would expect some elements of the Mycenaean population to join in the marauding and the migrating themselves. If the Akawash among the 'Sea Peoples' in Merneptah's reign were in fact Achaeans, that would be proof enough. Somewhat firmer, if still controversial, evidence comes from Cyprus. It was said at the end of Chapter 3 that, whereas the imports of Mycenaean pottery in the centuries before 1200 were not accompanied by any real migration into the island from Greece, about 1200 there is a marked change in the archaeological picture which implies an influx of immigrants. The masonry walls of Enkomi are perhaps the most noticeable novelty, but there is also an upswing in craftsmanship, in both metals and ivory, and there is the mysterious script (already mentioned). Unfortunately, no Cypriot writing survives from this, or the immediately succeeding, centuries, but the most plausible explanation for the survival in classical Cyprus of an Arcadian dialect and a script linked with Linear B is that they were brought there by Mycenaean Greeks about the year 1200. What then incites disagreement is the fact that in remarkably few years after the appearance of the new culture traits, the island was devastated, with immediate effects in the settlement pattern and the level of wealth and craftsmanship comparable to those we have already seen in Greece.[1] Again there

[1] Much of the controversy would probably disappear if the key archaeological finds could be dated very precisely round the pivotal year 1200.

is an 'if' in the picture. If Alasiya is correctly equated with Cyprus, there could be no doubt that this destruction was the work of the 'Sea Peoples' on their way to Egypt, as expressly stated in the Ramses account. It would then be tempting to imagine a first and considerable wave of Greek refugees, whose impact is seen in the new archaeological picture, followed within perhaps two decades by the destroying 'Sea Peoples'. But that would still leave the very difficult question of how refugees could have made such an impact in so short a time.

In Greece itself, one consequence of the new situation was that the separate communities turned in on themselves somehow. III C pottery was a direct outgrowth stylistically and technically from III B, but, unlike the latter, it quickly subdivided into local styles of marked diversity. Presumably this came about through the removal of the palaces as the controlling hand over the economy within their former power spheres, and through a considerable reduction in inter-regional communication and trade. Apart from pottery, the archaeological evidence for the next two or three centuries is very thin and unrevealing in any positive sense. Yet this very negative quality permits certain inferences. The population was smaller and very much poorer than before; that is to say not that the ordinary farmers and craftsmen were poorer, but that the upper classes were. There is no gainsaying the technical and artistic inferiority of the finds, the absence of treasure, and, above all, of large constructions, whether palatial, military or religious. Mycenaean society had been decapitated and those who remained, proceeded together with the new invading element,[1] to build a new kind of

---

[1] That some of the invaders remained in Greece is an assumption which it is impossible to prove. It is characteristic of this kind of combined invasion and migration that it leaves no archaeological record until it comes to rest somewhere permanently. Some scholars have sought evidence in the fact that the Bronze Age Greek practice of burying the dead was replaced in most districts by cremation. There is no denying that it would be very satisfactory if a link could be established with the 'urnfields', cemeteries of cremated corpses deposited in urns, first noticeable in central Europe in the thirteenth century, and

society. It is precisely this process which archaeology alone cannot illuminate very much. That it was a totally new society, however, is demonstrated later on, when writing returned to Greece and we begin to know something about the economy and the social and political organization.

The unavoidable concentration on material remains and technology should not be permitted to conceal the extent of the break that had occurred. Of course people went on farming and herding and making pottery and tools, using essentially the same techniques as before (but soon turning more and more to the new metal, iron, now available for the first time). They also continued to worship their gods and perform the necessary rituals, and presumably in this field of activity there was much continuity as well as change. But society was organized in a different way, it entered a very different path of development, and new values were created. The Bronze Age had come to an end.

---

then widely dispersed in large sections of the continent, including Italy. However, the change in Greece came slowly after 1200, and was not completed before about 1050. Furthermore, it was indicated in Chapter 2 that dramatic changes in methods of disposing of the dead are known to have occurred without the impetus of a new element in the population.

PART TWO

THE ARCHAIC AGE

7

The Dark Age

UNLESS life itself is destroyed in a region, there must always be continuity of some kind. In that sense, Greek history was a continuation of its Bronze Age prehistory. To make too much of that truism, however, is to put the stress in the wrong place and to overlook how fundamentally new the new society was to become. The Greeks of historical times had no tradition of a break and therefore no concept of a different civilization in the millennium before their own, although they did know in a vague and inaccurate way that other languages had once been spoken in Greece and the islands. Their 'heroic age', familiar to them from the Homeric poems and from much legendary material (such as the Oedipus story), was merely an early stage in Greek history. That is why Theseus could be credited with destroying the minotaur and with unifying Attica, both legendary actions, but one more appropriate to the Bronze Age, the other to the very different world of the Dark Age. Modern archaeology has discovered a prehistoric world never dreamed of by the Greeks of the historical era.

Archaeology brings to the forefront breakdown and decline about 1200 B.C., followed by poverty and a low quality of artistry and technology. What it reveals much less clearly, and in certain critical respects not at all, is that the centuries after 1200 point ahead, not only materially with the emergence of iron as the new and most advanced metal, but also socially, politically and culturally. The future of the Greeks lay not in palace-centred, bureaucratic states but in the new kind of society which was forged out of the impoverished communities that survived the great catastrophe. We cannot follow that process of growth in its formative stages, except in scattered hints strewn in the archaeological record and in later traditions, and we are not helped by the fact that in the contemporary written documents from Syria, Mesopotamia and Egypt there is no reference whatever to the Greeks. In the sense, therefore, that *we* grope in the dark, and in that sense only, is it legitimate to employ the convention of calling the long period in Greek history from 1200 to 800 a 'dark age'. And like the other 'ages' we are concerned with, subdivisions must be noted, one about 1050, a second in the course of the ninth century.

Regional variations make it difficult to present the archaeological picture of the Dark Age succinctly. True, a uniform dullness sets in everywhere (apart from an occasional find which is strikingly exceptional). Pictorial representation of human and animal figures is abandoned; there is no grandeur of scale, and hardly any building in stone at all; nor is there delicacy in the small objects, as gems are no longer manufactured. Luxury articles, all nonessential imports, virtually disappear: the absence of amber has already been noted, and the rare gold ornament indicates no more than a tomb robbery or a chance discovery of a Mycenaean hoard. Scarcely anything in the remains has religious associations we can grasp, apart, of course, from the fact itself that the dead were buried with a few objects of utility. There is little enough which reflects war or the warrior. For a century or a century and a half, everything still tends to look like 'debased' Mycenaean work. The pottery in particular maintains a continuity of style and technique, though Mycenaean III C and then 'sub-Mycenaean' ware had not only changed sufficiently to be differentiated from III B products, but also varied from place to place.

It is in the course of the eleventh century that genuine innovations first loom large in the archaeological record. There is 'protogeometric' pottery (Figure 4), most easily recognizable from the compass-drawn circles and half-circles painted with a multiple brush. Experts see it as a 'descendant' from the Mycenaean, but the style is different enough to warrant a new classification (unlike 'sub-Mycenaean'). New tools, weapons and small objects (such as long metal dress-pins in place of buttons, indicating a change in both men's and women's clothing) are increasingly made of iron instead of bronze. In the critical class of

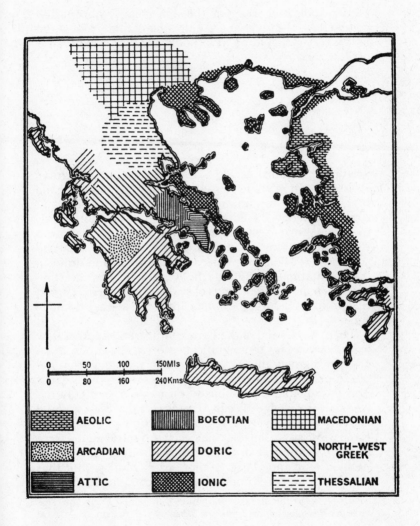

4 GREEK DIALECTS *c.* 400 B.C.

cutting tools and weapons the shift is fairly abrupt and complete, as the following simple table of finds from mainland Greece (excluding Macedonia) for the period 1050—900 shows:[1]

	Bronze	Iron
Swords	1	20+
Spearheads	8	30+
Daggers	2	8
Knives	0	15+
Axe-heads	0	4

There are, in most areas, changes not only in the grave structure but also in burial practices. Notable is the replacement of inhumation by cremation, completed in Athens, where the evidence is extensive and continuous, by about 1050.[2] All these changes were foreshadowed earlier in one way or another, and it would be wrong to suggest that about 1050 there was a sudden and uniform transformation throughout the Aegean world. Nevertheless, when the different kinds of evidence are taken together, a significant change becomes apparent at that point in time.[3]

Then, by the end of the same century, still another new feature emerges, the significance of which is far more obvious, namely the establishment by migrants from the Greek peninsula of small communities along the coast of Asia Minor and on the offshore islands. Eventually the whole western edge of Asia Minor became Greek, and the Aegean was converted for the first time into a Greek waterway, so to speak. The eastern settlements were grouped by dialect in three bands from north to south, Aeolic, Ionic and Doric, in that order (Map 4). But that required some three hundred years of complicated history

[1] From A. M. Snodgrass, 'Barbarian Europe and Early Iron Age Greece', *Proceedings of the Prehistoric Society*, 31 (1965), pp 229–240, at p. 231.

[2] Infants and very young children continued to be interred regularly, and not cremated.

[3] It is important to note that these dates are all archaeological, as explained in Chapter 1. Protogeometric pottery is pivotal in establishing the chronology.

which is largely lost to us—years of quarrelling and fighting with each other, and of ambiguous relations with the older inhabitants. We may suspect that few women were among the migrants, at least in the earlier days. In Miletus, writes Herodotus (I 146), the noblest of the colonists from Athens brought no women, 'but took Carian women, whose kinsmen they murdered. Because of the killing, the women laid down a law for themselves, which they swore an oath to observe and which they passed on to their daughters, never to dine with their husbands or to address them by name.' Just how Herodotus came to this story or what he was trying to explain is unclear, but in his own day intermarriage with Carians was a common practice in his native Halicarnassus. And we know (as Herodotus did not), thanks to recent and still preliminary archaeological investigation, that there were many separate migrations in small groups; that these were new settlements and not continuations or reinforcements of old Bronze Age or Mycenaean communities in Asia Minor (even where there was a return to previously occupied places, as at Miletus or Rhodes); that the first wave left Greece soon after the development of protogeometric pottery. Indeed, it is the discovery of quantities of protogeometric sherds in half a dozen or so sites which has enabled archaeologists to date the movements and to link some of the eastern sites with specific regions in Greece.[1] Aeolic and Ionic settlements were the earliest, the Doric somewhat later (not before 900, perhaps).

Exactly why any particular group chose to cross the Aegean *when* it did is anyone's guess, but there is no need to guess why they went where they did. The Asia Minor coast is a series of promontories with natural defences, backed by fertile river-valleys and plains, and in the eleventh, tenth and ninth centuries there were no strong powers or even

[1] The unexpected recent discovery (see *Illustrated London News* for 6 April, 1968) of Mycenaean III C, sub-Mycenaean and protogeometric sherds in Sardis, the eventual inland capital of Lydia, raises new questions. There may be a link with the refugee movement of about 1200, as in Cyprus and Tarsus, followed by trading connexions, rather than another case of an actual Greek migration of the kind we are considering.

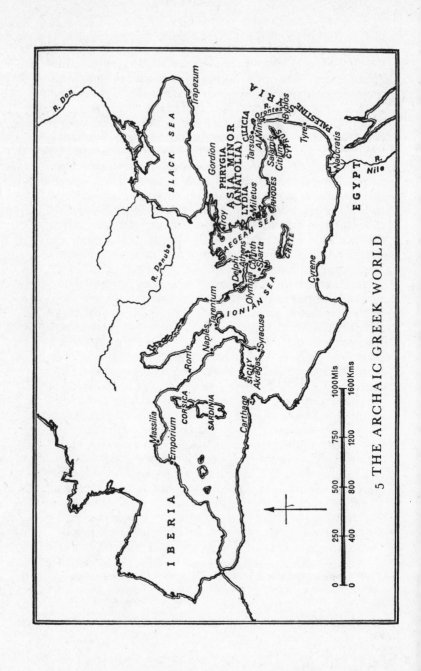

5 THE ARCHAIC GREEK WORLD

large populations to block new settlers from establishing themselves. One site—Old Smyrna, so called to differentiate it from the later city of Smyrna, modern Izmir, nearby—provides a picture of what these early communities came to look like: small, mean, cramped and huddled behind their fortified city-wall. At the end of the Dark Age, when, presumably, it had grown substantially from its earliest size, Old Smyrna counted no more than 500 small houses inside and outside the walls, representing a population of perhaps 2000.

This was also a 'dark age' as far as most of the native populations of western Asia Minor are concerned, and there is little on which to base a firm opinion about the relations between them and the Greek newcomers. It has been suggested that the Greeks were able to subjugate the people in their immediate neighbourhood and employ them as a dependent labour-force. This is a plausible guess—certainly Greek migrants did just that in historical times in Asia Minor, on the shores of the Black Sea, and in the west—but no more than that. We cannot even put names to the natives. The mysterious Carians were presumably there, though perhaps not yet the Lydians. Only the Phrygians have now come to light and they were in this early period too remote to be called neighbours. They came into Asia Minor across the Dardanelles at a time that was probably close to that of the earliest Greek migrations, but they were concentrated further inland. By the eighth century B.C., their greatest centre, Gordion, more than 200 miles from the Aegean coast, was large, rich and powerful, with a culture, partly inherited from the Hittites, technologically and materially more advanced than that of the Greeks. For the latter, Phrygia was the kingdom of Midas, whose touch turned everything to gold. Gordion was destroyed early in the seventh century by the Cimmerians sweeping in from the Russian steppes beyond the Caucasus, and that was the end of the Phrygian golden age. When we hear of Phrygians in classical Greek texts, it is as a major source of slaves for the Greeks, employed, for example, in the Athenian silver mines.

From the eighth century at the latest, Phrygian imports

and Phrygian artistic influences are visible not only in Greek Asia Minor but also in Greece proper, and there were close relations with the civilizations further east. The archaeologists have discovered what appear to be traces of the Hittite 'royal road' across Anatolia, which the Phrygians then maintained. That, however, was not the main route of eastern influence to the Greek world of the Dark Age, but the sea route from Syria, with Cyprus as a major intermediary. Contact between Greece and the Near East was never completely broken; it could not have been, if for no other reason than the imperative Greek need to import metal—copper, tin, and then, increasingly, iron—which at that time came largely, if not wholly, from the east.

Although Cyprus had been devastated by the 'Sea Peoples', copper mining almost certainly never stopped, and by the eleventh century the island was also important for its iron metallurgy, the influences of which are visible on the Greek mainland in weaponry. Significantly, the main Cypriot centres were henceforth to grow on the eastern and southeastern coasts, closest to Syria. Enkomi was replaced by nearby Salamis, perhaps originally a Greek foundation of about 1100, and in the tenth century the Phoenicians made Citium their centre there. In the centuries to come, every Near Eastern empire conquered Cyprus in turn—first the Assyrians, then the Egyptians, and finally the Persians—though they could not always retain control. The result was a hybrid civilization which it is difficult to classify. Although Greek was the language of the majority of the population, an unidentified pre-Greek tongue remained in existence as well as Phoenician (the earliest Cypriot document in that language, a curse tablet, is dated to about 900). The art became more Levantine than Greek, as exemplified by the newly discovered 'royal tombs' of Salamis of the eighth and seventh centuries.[1] By then kingship had disappeared in the Greek world, but it survived in Cyprus as long as the island retained any semblance of autonomy.

It was presumably the close eastern connexion (and

[1] V. Karageorghis, *Salamis in Cyprus, Homeric, Hellenistic and Roman* (London: Thames & Hudson 1969), chap. 3.

perhaps control) which enabled Cyprus to outstrip the Anatolian Greeks during the Dark Age. The discovery in excavations shortly before the last war of an ancient port at Al Mina, in the Orontes River delta in northern Syria (actually within the borders of Turkey today), brought to light one of the important link-posts on the Asiatic mainland. Cypriot and local pottery at Al Mina go back to the ninth century, and possibly earlier. By about 800, Greek pottery appears and then it becomes increasingly abundant, continuing after the Assyrian conquest of the area in the late eighth century. The source of the earliest Greek ware was not in Asia Minor but in Euboea and the Cyclades, later in Corinth and elsewhere. None of the evidence indicates what was traded in return, but there can be little doubt that metal was, as usual, a main Greek concern. The presence of so much Greek pottery suggests direct Greek participation—though it should be stressed that this was only a trading-post, not a permanent settlement of migrants as in Asia Minor—but it is not without relevance to recall that in the Homeric poems overseas trade was virtually a monopoly of 'Phoenicians', and that to Homer, as to Herodotus in the fifth century, 'Phoenicia' meant everything from the Cilician-Syrian border to Egypt.

No writing has been found at Al Mina and therefore its ancient name is unknown. It is just possible that it was the site of Posideion, according to Herodotus (III 91) the city which in his day was the northern boundary of one of the Persian provinces or satrapies. All that he could tell us about the past of Posideion was that it had been founded by one of the legendary Greek heroes, Amphilochus. And, in general, when the eastern Greeks finally came to write their history, which was not before the fifth century B.C., the earliest period was represented by little more than foundation stories built around individuals, and stories of isolated incidents, usually conflicts. They could offer no narrative going back beyond the sixth century, and they had no interest in a sustained account of social or institutional history. The picture they have left us is a schematic, sentimental reading back into the past of the values and claims of a later age, a 'mythical charter' for the present. Herodotus himself was uneasy. When he suggested (III 122) that Polycrates of Samos was the first Greek to seek a maritime empire, he explained that he was 'leaving aside Minos' and others like him, that Polycrates was the first 'in what is called the time of men'. We should phrase it as the first in historical, as distinct from mythical, times.

Our only check, archaeology, cannot cope with stories about individual founders or specific incidents. However, archaeology has exposed as false a fundamental element in the traditions about the early Ionian colonization, imagined to have been a single action, organized by and starting out from Athens, where many refugees from the Dorians had congregated, including men from Pylos under King Neleus. That Athens had a role in some of the Ionian settlements is certain, but little else stands up. The Greek antiquarians who put the story into writing more than 500 years afterwards had no notion of the great breakdown of about 1200 B.C., no idea of a Bronze Age, and therefore no sense of the very considerable time-span of the Dark Age. They did not, and could not, know that there had been a gap of perhaps 150 years between the destruction of Pylos (which was not the work of the 'Dorians') and the earliest movements across the Aegean, far too long for a crowd of Pylian refugees to wait in Athens, an inherently improbable situation anyway. And the single colonizing expedition is pure fiction, whereas the paramount role of Athens in the development and diffusion of protogeometric pottery, which is fact, was completely forgotten (and it is doubtful that the later Greeks would even have recognized this pottery as their own).

It is fruitless to pursue in detail the later Greek traditions about the Dark Age in Asia Minor. Nor is the possibility substantially greater for Greece proper, where the traditions down to 800 or 750 B.C. are of the same kind and quality. We must turn instead to our earliest written documentation, the Homeric *Iliad* and *Odyssey*, two epic poems, some 16,000 and 12,000 lines in length, respectively. What are we to make of them as sources of historical information? There is perhaps no question about the early Greeks which

provokes greater controversy and less agreement, and here
it is not possible to do more than state the position adopted
in this book.[1]

The two poems were composed in Ionia, the *Iliad*
perhaps in the middle of the eighth century, the *Odyssey* a
bit later, by two different poets working in the same
tradition. They were the culmination of a long experience
in oral poetry, practised by professional bards who
travelled widely in the Greek world. In the course of
generations they knit together many incidents and local
traditions, built round several main heroic themes, and
they employed a highly stylized and formalized, artificial
poetic language, in dialect basically Ionic but including
Aeolic and other elements. No doubt there were bards in
the Mycenaean world, too, but the tradition behind the
Homeric poems was essentially a Dark Age one (and its
existence provides an important corrective to judging the
period solely from its *material* impoverishment). It was a
tradition that deliberately looked back to a *lost* heroic age,
and there are aspects of their own world which the poets
successfully excluded. There is in the *Iliad* and *Odyssey* a
considerable, though by no means perfect, knowledge of
where the greatest Mycenaean centres had been located;
there is not a hint that Asia Minor was now rather thickly
settled by Greeks; there are no Dorians; there are indeed no
distinctions, whether in dialect or in institutions, within
the Greek world, other than differences in power. And
there are the great palaces of the heroes, filled with
'treasure' (*keimelion*). When Agamemnon was finally
persuaded to appease the wrath of Achilles, his offer
included (besides seven cities and a daughter to wife with a
great dowry) racehorses, captive women, 'seven tripods
that have never been on the fire and ten talents of gold and
twenty glittering cauldrons' and a shipload of bronze and
gold from the anticipated Trojan spoils (*Iliad* IX, 121–56).
The Dark Age possessed no treasure like that. Then, even
the warriors were allowed one sword or one lance-head

[1] In this chapter, our concern is with the society of the poems, not
with the narrative of the Trojan War and its aftermath. already discussed in the previous chapter.

after death, uncommonly both together; as time went on, indeed, arms of any kind became increasingly rare in the graves.

Thus far, one might imagine that the bards had transmitted, from generation to generation down to the eighth century, a recognizable picture of the late Mycenaean world. However, on closer analysis it turns out that their palaces are in structure and details not Mycenaean palaces (or any other known ones), that their understanding of the use of chariots in warfare has become uncertain, that the social system of the poems differs qualitatively from that of the Linear B tablets (and in particular from the palace economy recorded in the tablets), that the very terminology of administration and social structure has been radically altered. Even their 'realistic' accounts of treasure betray at least one remarkable anachronism. The dowries, racehorses and captive women of Agamemnon's offer of amends are timeless, or at least undatable, but not so the bronze 'tripods' and 'glittering cauldrons'. Although such objects existed in the Mycenaean world, they were rarities, whereas in the Dark Age they became notable treasures, above all to be dedicated to the gods, especially towards the end of the period, when the *Iliad* and *Odyssey* were composed. A few complete specimens and many fragments have been found in Olympia (*Plate IV*) and Delphi, a smaller number in Delos, Crete and Ithaca, isolated examples elsewhere.

There is also significant change in religious practices. The Mycenaean world buried its dead; the Homeric poems cremated them, without exception. Again a difference within the Dark Age itself must be noted. By about 1050 cremation of adults had become universal in most of the Greek world (with the curious exception of the Argolid), but 200 or 250 years later, inhumation returned to the mainland while cremation continued in Crete, the Cyclades, Rhodes and Ionia. The *Iliad* and *Odyssey* remain firmly anchored in the earlier Dark Age on this point, although the paraphernalia and rites of mourning can be illustrated from later Dark Age graves and from scenes on 'geometric' pottery after about 800. That was the period when human and animal figures returned to Greek art for the first time since the Mycenaean age, a revival which did not go so far as an early return to portrayal of the divine. There are no epiphanies, no ritual dances, no initiation scenes; there are very few figures, either in sculpture or in the decorations on pottery, that one can imagine as gods even on a broad interpretation. This rarity in the plastic arts of the anthropomorphic spirit that dominates the Homeric poems is surprising (especially in contrast to the innumerable idealized Zeuses, Apollos and Aphrodites of later Greek art).

In sum, the Homeric poems retain a certain measure of Mycenaean 'things'—places, arms and weapons, chariots —but little of Mycenaean institutions or culture. The break had been too sharp. As the pre-1200 civilization receded into the past, the bards could not avoid 'modernizing' the behaviour and the social background of their heroes. All in all, there is an inner coherence in the way social institutions emerge from a study of the *Iliad* and *Odyssey*, despite the anachronisms at either end of the time-scale. That picture, it is suggested, is in general one of the Dark Age, and on the whole of the earlier half of that age, painted as a poet does and not a historian or chronicler, not precise or always accurate, surely exaggerated in scale, but not therefore a purely imaginary one.

The world of Agamemnon and Achilles and Odysseus was one of petty kings and nobles, who possessed the best land and considerable flocks, and lived a seignorial existence, in which raids and local wars were frequent. The noble household (*oikos*) was the centre of activity and power. How much power depended on wealth, personal prowess, connexions by marriage and alliance, and retainers. There is no role assigned to tribes or other large kinship groups. In the twenty years Odysseus was away from Ithaca, the nobles behaved scandalously towards his family and his possessions; yet his son Telemachus had no body of kinsmen to whom to turn for help, nor was the community fully integrated, properly organized and equipped to impose sanctions. Telemachus' claims as

Odysseus' heir were acknowledged in principle, but he lacked the power to enforce them. The assassination of Agamemnon by his wife Clytaemnestra and her paramour Aegisthus placed an obligation of vengeance on his son Orestes, but otherwise life in Mycenae went on unchanged, except that Aegisthus ruled in Agamemnon's place. The king with power was judge, lawgiver and commander, and there were accepted ceremonies, rituals, conventions and a code of honour by which nobles lived, including table fellowship, gift-exchange, sacrifice to the gods and appropriate burial rites. But there was no bureaucratic apparatus, no formalized legal system or constitutional machinery. The power equilibrium was delicately balanced; tension between king and nobles was chronic, struggles for power frequent.

Telemachus, it is true, summoned a meeting of the assembly in Ithaca to hear his complaint against the noble 'suitors'. The assembly listened to both sides and took no action, which is what the assembly always did in the two poems. In general, the silence of the people is the most challenging difficulty presented to the historian by the poems. They are there all the time, even in the battles, but as a vague mass whose exact status is unclear. Some, chiefly captive women, are called slaves, but they do not appear to be worse off than the others. A few specialists—seers, bards, metalworkers, woodworkers, physicians—have a higher status. There is seafaring and a vital concern for trade, more exactly for the import of copper, iron, gold and silver, fine cloths and other luxuries. Even chieftains are permitted to go on expeditions for such purposes, but generally trade and merchandising seem to be the business of foreigners, chiefly Phoenicians. To be called a merchant was a grave insult to Odysseus; men of his class exchanged goods ceremonially or they took it by plunder. In part, all this vagueness about the ordinary people can be attributed to the poets' deliberate concentration on the heroic deeds of heroes. But perhaps it is also to be explained by the absence, in reality, of the sharp status categories of later societies, in particular of neat categories of 'freedom' and 'bondage'. The fundamental class-line between noble and non-noble is clear enough. Above and below that line the distinctions appear blurred, and perhaps they really were.

It would be idle to pretend that this provides the basis for a *history* of the Dark Age. All that can be suggested is that, following the elimination of the rulers of the Mycenaean world and with them of the whole power structure they headed, society had to reorganize itself with new arrangements and new values appropriate to the new material and social situation, in which migrants were presumably one factor to be reckoned with. If, as is probable but not provable, the destruction of the Mycenaean world also involved internal social upheavals, that would also have influenced the shape of the new arrangements. What happened in the centuries immediately following could not have been the same everywhere, despite the Homeric image of uniformity. In Asia Minor from the beginning (as in all subsequent Greek migrations to new areas), the settlements were small territorial units around an urban core. Judging from the archaeology, similar units existed in some Aegean islands and they gradually developed on the Greek mainland as well. The poets assume them to be the rule, but still in their day and for several centuries to come, whole areas of Greece—Thessaly and Aetolia, for example—in fact lacked urban centres and were loosely organized agrarian and pastoral societies. What was apparently uniform, however, was the class structure suggested by the poems, with an aristocratic upper class and a king or chieftain who was a bit more than 'first among equals'. How much more (or less) was a personal matter in each case, and, as we know from other indications, by the time the *Iliad* and *Odyssey* were composed the 'equals' had dispensed with the king almost everywhere and replaced monarchy by aristocracy. In some shadowy way, the common people also had an existence as a corporate body (whomever 'the people', the *demos*, may have included), but not as a political force in any constitutional sense.

Curiously, although the poets were conscious of a common bond uniting all the Greeks, a bond of language, religion and way of life (but not, either then or later, of a political bond or of a reluctance to war with each other), neither the *Iliad* nor the *Odyssey* refers to them by the name which has been theirs from at least the eighth century to our own day. They are Hellenes and their world is Hellas; 'their world', not in antiquity 'their country', because they were never politically united and therefore Hellas was an abstraction much like Christendom in the Middle Ages or Islam today. In the Homeric poems the Greeks have three different names, Achaeans, Argives and Danaans, the first two of which lived on as the names of specific localities in Greece (Map 6) while the third disappeared from use. It is virtually certain, however, that Hellas and Hellene were already current in the eighth century, and probably also the genealogies which were inevitably invented to explain the historical divisions according to dialect, 'race' or political organization: Hellen, son of Deucalion, had three sons named Dorus, Xuthus (father of Ion) and Aeolus, and so on. In the eighth century, too, embryonic pan-Hellenic institutions were already in existence, notably certain oracles and the Olympic Games.

The eighth century, finally, saw the return of writing to the Greeks, in the form of the alphabet borrowed with modification from the Phoenicians. This fact the Greek tradition had right (though they had no idea of the date). We are in the position to pin the source down to the North Semitic script, and specifically the cursive writing used in business activity rather than the monumental characters of, for example, Byblos. Al Mina may have been the point of contact and diffusion, though that is only a guess, and the first borrowers were perhaps people from Euboea, Crete and Rhodes, more or less independently of each other, from whom the art then spread, by a complicated network of routes, to all the Greek communities. Neither the immediate reasons why the alphabet was acquired when it was (probably before 750) nor why it spread so rapidly are well understood. A long time was to go by before the Greeks made serious use of this new skill for chronicles or for religious texts, two of the chief uses of writing in the ancient Near East. Originally the Greeks seem to have concentrated on poetry and on what may be

6 ARCHAIC GREECE
AND THE ASIA MINOR COAST

called labelling and mnemonic purposes, that is, inscribing names on pottery, gravestones and the like, on the one hand, and easing the burden of memory, on the other hand, by writing down lists that merited public notice and remembrance, such as Olympic victors.

The Homeric poems, in sum, looked back to the Dark Age and even a bit beyond, but they were composed at the beginning of a new era. By convention the next period (800–500 B.C. in round numbers) is known as 'archaic', a

85

word taken from the history of art, and more narrowly of sculpture (as is the term 'classical' for the succeeding age). It is with Archaic Greece that the rest of this book will be concerned.

8

Archaic Society and Politics

Two phenomena which mark the Archaic Age are the emergence and slow development of the characteristically Greek community-structure, the *polis* (conventionally and not very aptly translated 'city-state'), and the vast diffusion of Hellas in the course of about two hundred years, from the southeastern end of the Black Sea almost to the Atlantic Ocean.

It has already been noted that in the Dark Age the community had only a shadowy existence as a political organism. How the shadow acquired substance is a process we cannot trace, but at the heart lay the creation of institutions which subjected even the most powerful men to *formal* organs and rules of authority. This was no simple task; tension between the organs of the community and the power drives of ambitious individuals remained a disturbing factor in Greek society not only in the archaic period but also in the classical. One step was the elimination of kingship,[1] a step which was curiously unnoticed in Greek legends and traditions. The contrast in this respect with early Roman history could scarcely be greater. In time, the Romans developed a very full and detailed story of the reigns of their kings, each in turn, climaxed by the expulsion of the last of them, Tarquinius Superbus in 509.[2] The abolition of kingship was a story of a revolt from Etruscan overlordship, and that explains something of its attraction and its tenacity in Roman legends. The Greeks lacked such a stimulus. And their silence about this aspect of their past suggests that anyway, despite the Agamemnons and

[1] One survival, in Sparta, will be considered in Chapter 9. It should also be noted that the word *basileus*, 'king', remained in use for such officials as the magistrates in charge of religious affairs in Athens, without any implication of royal status.

[2] See, for example, the first two books of Livy's history (available in the Penguin volume of Livy entitled *The Early History of Rome*).

Ajaxes of the Homeric poems, their real Dark Age rulers were petty chieftains within a framework of 'many kings', whose disappearance from the scene was undramatic and unmemorable. Without them, the nobles were compelled to formalize the previously informal advisory bodies we see in action in the Homeric poems. So there arose councils and offices (which we call 'magistracies', borrowing the word from the Latin), with more or less defined prerogatives and responsibilities, and with a machinery for selection and rotation, all confined within the closed group of the landowning aristocracy.

These communities were small and independent (unless subjected by force). Following the normal Mediterranean residential pattern, they had an 'urban' centre, for a long time no more than a village, where the wealthier people tended to reside. The town square, an open space, was reserved: eventually it was flanked by civic and religious buildings—the temple made its appearance as a regular feature from about 800 B.C.—but easy access was carefully maintained so that the people could all be assembled when required. That was the agora in its original sense, a 'gathering-place', long before shops and stalls began to encroach, so that the common 'market-place' translation of the word *agora* is rarely quite right and sometimes just wrong. Often there was also an acropolis (if the terrain was suitable), a high point to serve as a citadel for defence. Essentially town and country were conceived as a unit, not, as was common in medieval cities, as two antagonistic elements. This was built into the language, which equated the community with the people and not with a place. An ancient Greek could express the idea of Athens as a community or as a political unit only by saying 'the Athenians'. The word 'Athens' was very rarely used in any sense other than geographical; one travelled to Athens but one made war with the Athenians. Of course, the tempo of development among these farflung autonomous communities was very uneven and there were considerable variations in the end-product. The community of the eighth and seventh centuries had a long way to go before it became the classical *polis*. Nevertheless, the embryo was there in the early

Archaic period.

The fragmentation which characterized Hellas is partly explained by geography. Much of the terrain in Greece proper is a chequer-board of mountains and small plains or valleys, tending to isolate each pocket of habitation from the other. In Asia Minor the coastal region had roughly the same structure and therefore encouraged a comparable settlement-pattern. The Aegean islands were also mountainous and they were mostly very small. But the geography is not a sufficient explanation, and especially not of later Greek developments. It cannot explain, for example, why the whole of Attica was politically united whereas neighbouring Boeotia, which is not much larger, contained twelve independent city-states who on the whole successfully resisted the efforts of the largest, Thebes, to dominate them; nor why a tiny island like Amorgos had three separate *poleis* right through the classical era; nor, above all, why the Greeks transplanted the small community to Sicily and southern Italy, where both the geography and self-preservation should have argued for embracing much larger territories within single political structures. Clearly there was something far greater at stake, a conviction that the *polis* was the only proper structure for civilized life, a conviction which Aristotle (*Politics* 1253a7–9) summed up, in the last days of Greek independence, when he defined man as a *zoön politikon*, a being destined by nature to live in a *polis*.

Land communication from one pocket to another was slow and cumbersome, sometimes actually impossible in the face of resistance. Inland waterways were almost wholly lacking, and therefore the sea became the normal Greek highway, even for relatively short distances wherever possible. In antiquity the Greeks became the people of the sea *par excellence*, and yet their attitude to it was notably ambiguous: it was the home of those pleasant nymphs, the Nereids, but it was ruled over by Poseidon, whom men feared and appeased but never loved. Nevertheless, when they were forced into a continuous movement of expansion, from the middle of the eighth century, they took to the sea, going west and northeast. By the end of the Archaic Age, Hellas covered an enormous area, from the northern, western and southern shores of the Black Sea, through western Asia Minor and Greece proper (with the Aegean islands) to much of Sicily and southern Italy, then continuing west along both shores of the Mediterranean to Cyrene in Libya and to Marseilles and some Spanish coastal sites, Wherever they went, they settled on the edge of the sea, not in the hinterland.

The sea was not the only common environmental feature of these farflung regions. Ecologically they shared (with a few exceptions) what we popularly call a 'Mediterranean' climate and vegetation, permitting and even inducing an outdoor existence still familiar in our day. Summers are hot and sunny, winters are tolerable and usually free from snow on the shores and in the plains, olives and grapes grow freely, flowers abound, the plains produce cereals and vegetables, the sea is rich in fish, and there is adequate pasture on the hillsides (rich in places), at least for the smaller animals. Nothing is as a rule luxuriant, and therefore agriculture and pasturage need constant attention, but on the other hand the requirements of housing and especially of warmth, can be met by fairly primitive means. Only metals and wood suitable for such purposes as shipbuilding cause serious difficulties from short supply: they are available only in restricted, and sometimes rather distant, localities. Fresh water may also be a problem, hence the stress in legend and reality on springs and fountains.

Schematically the Greek 'colonization' movement may be conceived as two long waves (not counting the earlier settlement of Asia Minor). The western one began about 750 B.C. and continued in full swing until the middle of the next century, with a secondary wave going on for about another century, when the process was essentially completed. Migration to the northeast began before 700 with settlements in the Thracian region, in nearby islands such as Thasos and in the Troad in Asia Minor, followed from about 650 with further movement into the Hellespont area and then along both shores of the Black Sea, not stopping until the end of the sixth century, at the mouth of the Don on the north coast and at Trapezus (now Trebizond) at the southeastern end. Ancient accounts of these movements are not very helpful. One reasonably sober example, the accepted story of the foundation of Syracuse in Sicily, as repeated by the geographer Strabo (VI 2, 4), reads like this:

> Archias, sailing from Corinth, founded Syracuse about the same time that Naxos and Megara [also in Sicily] were established. They say that when Myscellus and Archias went to Delphi to consult the oracle, the god asked whether they preferred wealth or health. Archias chose wealth and Myscellus health, and the oracle then assigned Syracuse to the former to found, and Croton [in Southern Italy] to the latter.... On his way to Sicily, Archias left a part of the expedition to settle the island now called Corcyra [modern Corfu].... The latter expelled the Liburni who occupied it and established a settlement. Archias, continuing on his journey, met some Dorians ... who had separated from the settlers of Megara; he took them with him and together they founded Syracuse.

Such mythical overtones and the stress on a few individuals and their quarrels, rather than on the broader social aspects, are characteristic of most of the traditions. On the other hand, these accounts are more 'historical' than the still vaguer and more confused ones about the drift to Asia Minor early in the Dark Age. Whereas the earlier migrations were probably more in the nature of chancy, haphazard flights, what was now happening was an organized shift of population, though still in small numbers; group emigration systematically arranged by the 'mother-cities'.

The common Greek word for such a new settlement abroad, *apoikia*, connotes 'emigration' and lacks the implication of dependence inherent in our 'colony'. As a rule, each *apoikia* was from the outset, and by intention, an independent community, retaining sentimental and often religious, ties with its 'mother-city', but not a subject either economically or politically. Indeed, their independence helped preserve friendly relations with their old homes on the whole, free as they were from the irritations and conflicts commonly aroused under colonial conditions. The designation 'mother-city' it should be added, was often a slightly arbitrary choice; many of the new foundations were established by settlers joining together from more than one place in the old Greek world.

According to the commonly accepted chronological scheme, based on archaeology and Greek antiquarian efforts, the earliest colony was Cumae near Naples shortly before 750 B.C. (more precisely, the island now known as Ischia, from which Cumae was then founded), settled from Chalcis and Eretria, the two leading cities of Euboea (active at the same time at Al Mina in the Levant). Chalcis was also the mother-city of Sicilian Zancle (later Messina), of Rhegium on the Italian side of the straits, and of Naxos, Leontini and Catania (Katane in Greek) in eastern Sicily, all traditionally founded by 730. They were joined in Zancle by other Euboeans, in Rhegium by Messenian exiles, and in Leontini by Megarians. Syracuse was founded at the same time by Corinthians and unspecified 'other Dorians'; Sybaris in southern Italy in about 720 by men from Achaea with a sprinkling from Troezen in the Peloponnese; Gela in southern Sicily in 688 by Cretans and Rhodians. Thereafter foundations were further complicated by 'inner' migrations, as some colonies became mother-cities in turn, while emigrants continued to come from the east. Thus, Himera was established about 650 from Zancle with a contingent of Syracusan exiles; Selinus between 650 and 630 from Megara Hyblaea in eastern Sicily; Cyrene about 630 from the Aegean island of Thera; Massalia (Marseilles) about 600 by Phocaeans from Asia Minor; and Akragas (modern Agrigento) in 580 from Gela together with migrants coming directly from the latter's own motherland, Rhodes.

This list is not complete and none of the traditional dates is secure. Enough has been said to indicate the chronology of the movement, which has been archaeologically substantiated in its general outline, to underscore the way the settlements clung to the sea, and to reveal the number, diversity and geographical spread of the Greek communities involved. There is no need to repeat with a catalogue of the north Aegean and Black Sea foundations, for which both the literary and the archaeological evidence is much poorer. Settlement on the Thracian coast of the Aegean Sea began late in the eighth century, and again the cities of Euboea were in the vanguard, as shown by the name of the promontory Chalcidice (from Chalcis). Soon other Aegean islands came into the picture, Paros, Rhodes, and above all Chios. And then, as the movement went beyond the Aegean coast to the shores of the Black Sea, Miletus became the dominant mother-city (followed by Megara). If all the references to Milesian activity were taken too literally, that city itself would have been totally depopulated, and that is further proof of the restricted role of a 'mother-city'.

The lands to which the Greeks migrated, both east and west, were all inhabited, by a variety of peoples at different levels of development, that is to say, by people with different interests in the newcomers and different capacities of resistance. The Etruscans of central Italy were strong enough to stop Greek expansion at a line drawn from the Bay of Naples, and sufficiently advanced to borrow from the Greeks their alphabet, much of their art, and elements of their religion. The Sicels, however, like the Thracians or the Scythians in the north Aegean and Black Sea areas, were less advanced technically and socially. Some were apparently reduced to a semi-servile labour force, though the evidence is thin and confused. Others were pushed inland, where they maintained an uneasy and complicated relationship with the Greeks in the following centuries.

A study of the list of mother-cities (and of those which seem to have taken no part in colonization) shows that there was little correlation between type of community and colonizing city. In particular, there is nothing in the list to justify the once widely held view that the colonizing activity was *chiefly inspired* by commercial interests. Emphasis on the words 'chiefly inspired' is important. The intention is not to deny the commercial aspect of colonization altogether, in particular, the oft repeated need for metals. The island of Ischia, the first western settlement, had some iron, and anyway it was a gateway to the relatively rich ore-bearing regions of central Italy. Foundations on both sides of the Straits of Messina soon followed, evidently to control that narrow roadway to the western Italian coast. The first settlers seemed to know where they were headed, and the information could have come only from traders who had already been in the area. When this is said, however, it explains very little of the centuries-long movement of dispersion. Sicily, for example, had no metal and little else to attract Greek merchants, except in occasional ventures, and the same was true of the Black Sea hinterland. Archaeological evidence of Greek activity earlier than the first colonists is almost impossible to find. In the end, the central question is that of the motivation of the men who actually migrated, who left their homes in Greece, the islands or Asia Minor, to settle permanently in unfamiliar, and sometimes hostile, regions, essentially independent of their mother-cities from the start. They were not the same people as the traders, who did not abandon their home-bases, and so their interests were far from identical. Nor did merchants constitute a significant element in the migrants who followed to join the original settlers, or in the secondary colonies, such as Himera and Akragas, which in time split off from the earlier ones.

The distinction is emphasized by the small number of genuine trading-posts which were eventually established, such as the places called Emporium (which in Greek means literally 'trading-station' or 'market-centre') in Spain (now Ampurias) and at the mouth of the River Don; or the very interesting settlement at Naucratis in the Nile Delta, where the Pharaohs concentrated the representatives of a number of Greek states, chiefly in Asia Minor, who conducted trade with Egypt. The small number of these posts is revealing, as well as their relatively late foundation—Spanish Emporium was set up by Massalia, which was itself not founded before 600; Naucratis can be dated somewhat earlier than Massalia, whereas Russian Emporium was substantially later. But the most decisive point is that these were at the outset not proper Greek *poleis*, but, like Al Mina before them, meeting-points between the Greek world and the non-Greek, whereas all the other new settlements—to be counted in the dozens and eventually in the hundreds—were, from the beginning, Greek communities in all respects. That meant, above all, that they were basically agrarian settlements, established by men who had come in search of land. They settled near the sea and they welcomed good anchorage, but that was a subordinate consideration. Hence, numerous as were the Greek communities in southern Italy, there was none at the best harbour on the east coast, the site of Roman Brundisium (modern Brindisi). Hence, too, the aristocracy of Syracuse, which became the greatest of the new communities in the west, were called *gamoroi*, which means literally 'those who divided the land'.

In the final analysis, the one feature which all the mother-cities had in common was a condition of crisis severe enough to induce the mobilization of the resources required for so difficult a venture as an overseas transplantation—ships, armour and weapons, presumably tools, seed and supplies—and to create the necessary psychology as well. Behind the traditional stories of personal feuds, quarrels and murders which the later Greeks associated with some of the individual foundations, there lies a deeper and broader social conflict. One must not exaggerate the spirit of Viking adventurism in Archaic Greece.

A tantalizingly brief passage in Herodotus (IV 153) about the foundation of Cyrene from Thera gives us a clue, with the help of an early fourth-century inscription from Cyrene which purports to be the text of the pact of the first settlers.[1] What Herodotus says is this: 'The Therans decided to send out one brother from among brothers,

---

[1] The text and a translation of the inscription (*Supplementum epigraphicum graecum* IX 3) will be found in A. J. Graham, *Colony and Mother City in Ancient Greece* (Manchester University Press; New York, Barnes and Noble, 1964), pp. 224–6. The colony concerned was not the city of Cyrene itself, but a slightly earlier settlement on an offshore island.

selected by lot, from each of the seven districts of the island, and that Battos should be their leader and king. On these terms they dispatched two fifty-oared ships.' The inscription adds that the penalty for refusing to go was death and confiscation of property, and that volunteers were also accepted. Numbers were therefore small—two hundred at the most—and no women were included, with reminds us of the suggestion already made about the first movement into Asia Minor, that the earliest migrants took their wives from among the natives where they settled. And there was compulsion, although families with only sons seem to have been exempt. Why such pressure? We are not told. For Herodotus and for the people who later inscribed the 'pact' in Cyrene itself, the story is all tied up with orders from Apollo at Delphi and with a sanction for the Battiad dynasty which had seized power in Cyrene. That takes us back to the mythical explanations characteristic of most of the foundation stories. But the factual core remains, and though we do not know the precise situation, we cannot doubt the existence in Thera in the middle of the seventh century B.C. of a relative excess of population, and hence of the potential, if not yet the reality, of social conflict. Nor that the same was the case wherever active colonizing was being fostered, and probably often compelled.

Social conflict was rooted in the nature of aristocratic society and the ways it developed in the course of the Dark Age. Slowly increasing wealth and technical skills are demonstrable in the archaeology, and also, at the end of the period, a considerable rise in population. This is now being documented for the first time, as Greek archaeologists begin to concern themselves with such matters as demography and settlement patterns. But there are puzzles. In Argos and especially in Athens there appears to have been a population explosion at the very moment when the colonization process was intiated;[1] yet neither Argos nor Athens took part. On the other hand, Corinth, a leading colonizer, was still only a large village linked to other villages and

[1] See R Hägg, *Die Gräber der Argolis* (Uppsala Univ. 1974), pt. II ch. 1. A. M. Snodgrass, *Archaeology and the Rise of the Greek State* (Cambridge Inaugural Lecture 1977).

clusters of houses. If it had become overpopulated, that was 'not in the sense that available land was overbuilt, but by the system of land tenure'.[1]

With the elimination of kings in all but name, the aristocracy seems to have closed ranks, to have controlled much of the land (and in particular the best land), and to have created political instruments for monopolizing power. The stress on genealogies in the later traditions, with every noble 'family' claiming a divine or 'heroic' ancestor, is a certain sign of the tendency towards an exclusive aristocracy of 'blood'. Their wealth gave them a military monopoly for a long time. Metal was scarce and expensive, particularly the iron for swords and spearheads. About the middle of the eighth century, there came innovations in helmets, body armour and weapons, partly inspired from both central Europe and the east. Within another hundred years or so, the full panoply was being regularly worn, from helmet to greaves, and that was far beyond the reach of anyone without means. Wealth was also essential for horse-breeding, now important with the rise of the cavalry, a peculiarly aristocratic military arm throughout history. The place of cavalry in Archaic Greece is obscure and some historians tend to dismiss it as necessarily insignificant on Greek terrain. It cannot be denied, however, that horses and horsemen are very prominent in the painted pottery of the period; that such later Greek writers as Aristotle laid great stress on cavalry; that it was the Greek migrants who brought the cavalry to Italy; or that the ruling aristocracy of Euboea were called the Hippobotai, the 'horse-feeders', as late as the time of Herodotus (V 77). At the least, we must accept the value of cavalry in raiding and as a way of giving heavily armed fighters mobility in reaching a battlefield.

The aristocracy also used their wealth to forge bonds of patronage and obligation with commoners. It must be admitted that the status of the mass of these peasants, craftsmen and seafarers is unknown to us except in nebulous terms. Apart from such classes as the Spartan helots

[1] C. Roebuck, 'Some Aspects of Urbanization in Corinth'. *Hesperia* 41 (1972) 96–127.

(discussed in Chapter 9), the question remains open whether, and to what extent, the bulk of the labour force in the fields and pastures and in the noble households were free or half-free; or whether, indeed, such concepts are yet applicable in any meaningful way. Genuine slaves were to be found, captive women and fewer men, but the widespread reliance on chattels, on human beings who were property in the strict sense, was a phenomenon of the classical and post-classical periods, and therefore will not hold our attention in this book. But that does not imply that the lower classes were 'free' in our sense, or in a sense a fifth-century Athenian would have understood. Although they no doubt had personal and property rights that were protected by custom, and though they may still have been summoned to an assembly from time to time (as in the Homeric poems), it is more than probable that they were also tied in other respects, such as in an obligation to pay over a portion of their produce or to give an amount of unpaid labour, possibly even in a restriction on the right to move freely from their plot of land or their crafts. Perhaps this is the same kind of status that the Roman tradition about their own earliest era implied when the term 'clients' was used (not to be confused with the watered down meaning of the word in later periods).

We must allow further for 'declassed' aristocratic and for a middle class of relatively prosperous, but non-aristocratic, farmers with a sprinkling of merchants, shippers and craftsmen. Their origin and history may be obscure, but they make their appearance in the fragments of lyric poetry that begin about 650 B.C. and they were the major factor in the most important military innovation in all Greek history, at about the same time. Once the panoply had been sufficiently refined, it was only a matter of decades before some commander—possibly the half-legendary Pheidon of Argos—saw the possibility of organizing heavily armed infantrymen, called hoplites, into a close formation in close ranks. Its advantages over the much looser organization of the aristocratic warriors were so great that by the end of the seventh century, the phalanx had become the normal formation in the Greek world.

Furthermore, the advantages were enhanced by the simple device of increasing the levy, with profound social consequences. Hoplite arms and armour, which each soldier was normally required to provide from his own resources, were expensive. The innovation was therefore not a democratization of the army (that never occurred among the Greeks, except in a way in those states, such as Athens, which in the classical period used their navies, largely manned by the poorer classes, as a main military arm). However, the phalanx for the first time gave the commoners of more substantial means an important military function. It is tempting to link the disappearance of arms from the graves with this development, since arms no longer signified exclusive social status. On a less symbolic level, a place in the phalanx eventually led to demands for a share in political authority.

All classes thus found themselves involved in social conflict, or *stasis* (the generic Greek word), in varying combinations and alliances. Within the aristocracy itself, squabbling for honour and power was normal; the creation of formal institutions of political administration merely changed the conditions under which it went on. One need mention only the insistent Athenian tradition that the Alcmaeonid house were always breaking ranks and going their own way politically, or the monopoly of power achieved by the Bacchiads in Corinth. Then there were the wealthier among the the outsiders, demanding a share in the prerogatives, a demand which obviously became more insistent and effective once they attained military weight in the hoplite phalanx. And finally there were the poor, the mass of the working farmers, whose position seems to have worsened with the general increase in wealth and prosperity. A growing population was itself a danger, if not an outright evil: much of Greece and the Aegean islands simply could not support a large population on the soil. The seventh-century poet Hesiod not only advises late marriage (at the age of thirty) but adds the following (*Works and Days* 376–8, 695–7): 'There should be an only son, to feed his father's house, for so wealth will increase in

the home; but if you leave a second son you should die old.'[1]
Furthermore, a rising standard of living among the
wealthier classes will have led to greater pressure on the
lower classes, through a need for a larger and more
diversified labour force or through an expansion of their
holdings even into poorer and more marginal land. In the
end, as Aristotle wrote in his *Constitution of Athens* (II 1–2),
'there was civil strife between the nobles and the people for
a long time' because 'the poor, with their wives and
children, were enslaved to the rich' and 'had no political
rights'.

That lapidary statement is oversimplified, with its loose
use of the word 'enslaved', and too schematic. Nor are we in
a position to say how universal the *stasis* had become.
Nevertheless, the tradition of widespread demands for
redistribution of land and cancellation of debts was no
fiction.[2] Nor is it false to stress the aristocratic monopoly in
the administration of justice (and of the priestly functions). Hesiod is pointed enough about the 'gift-
devouring judges' of his day (*Works and Days* 263–4). For
the lower classes, unlike their betters, economic demands
and a plea for justice took precedence over claims to political rights. The search for justice explains another facet of
the tradition as we have it, namely, the role of the wise lawgiver. Law in the hands of a traditional and closed aristocracy, self-perpetuating and secretive, in a world which was
just learning how to write things down, was a powerful
weapon, and increasingly an intolerable one. There could be
no justice, rose the cry, until the law became public knowledge and its administration open and equitable. Inevitably the men who were charged with this task when the
demand became sufficiently insistent—such as Solon in
Athens, Charondas of Catania and Zaleucus of Locri in the
west—were reformers as well as codifiers. Lacking precedents, they invented freely, in a sort of compulsory originality which characterized every aspect of Archaic Greek life
and culture. This can hardly be overstated. The political

[1] Translated by H. G. Evelyn-White in the Loeb Classical Library
(Cambridge, Mass., Harvard University Press; London, Heinemann).
[2] See the account of Solon in Chapter 10.

structure, made up of magistrates, councils and, eventually, popular assemblies, was a free invention. Some myths and cult practices may have been borrowed from the east; the combination was original, the literary formulations, as early as Hesiod's *Theogony*, wholly so, as well as the very notion itself that a poet, lacking a priestly vocation, had the right to systematize the myths about the gods. Even the phalanx was a new creation, whatever the foreign source of parts of the hoplite's panoply.

Two points about these archaic lawgivers need special mention. One is their self-reliance. They all agreed that justice came from the gods, but rarely did they claim a divine mission or divine guidance. Appeals to the oracle at Delphi may have helped seal their work with a sort of divine blessing, as similar requests had occasionally been made to approve a proposal for colonization. But the sequence was almost always the same: measures were formulated first, then Delphi was consulted. This ambivalence remained characteristic of the Greek community for centuries. Religious activity was frequent and ubiquitous; later ages even invented Delphic oracles to make up for the many failures in the past to bother to consult Apollo; divine authority over, and interference in, the lives of men and communities were accepted as a part of the nature of things. Yet at the same time, the community found the inspiration and justification for its actions in itself, in human terms.

The second point is the acceptance by the lawgivers of human inequality. Justice was not equated with egalitarianism or democracy at this stage. Solon wrote, 'I gave the common people such privilege as is sufficient.' As to those in power, he continued, 'I saw to it that they should suffer no injustice. I stood covering both parties with a strong shield, permitting neither to triumph unjustly' (quoted by Aristotle, *Constitution of Athens* XII 1.) It is anachronistic to see even in Solon a democratic personality. The common people, the *demos*,[1] as a genuine political force may have lain just beneath the surface by the

[1] There is an ambiguity in the Greek *demos*: it may mean 'the people as a whole' or 'the common people', depending on the context.

beginning of the sixth century; popular sovereignty was not yet an issue.

What Solon's words serve to remind us is that the economic, juridical and political developments in Archaic Greece went on through a long period of struggle, confused, uneven, not continuous, but at the critical moments quite fierce. At first the opportunity to send out a sector of the population to new foundations served as a safety-valve. But the time finally came—and the middle of the seventh century seems to have been the turning-point in many areas—when external solutions no longer were available or no longer sufficed. The *stasis* flared up sharply, factious and ambitious individuals seized the opportunity to their own advantage, and there arose the specifically Greek institution of the tyrant. We do not know that the archaic tyrants ever called themselves that, but in any event the label came to be applied generically to a class of men who acquired autocratic power in their city-state. Eventually, too, the label took on an unfailingly pejorative overtone. Then the Greeks, looking back to the age of tyranny, coloured its history to suit their new moral condemnation, though they never wholly concealed the fact that individual tyrants varied greatly, that some had even ruled benevolently and well.

It is impossible to understand Greek tyranny without first making an effort to free the mind from the connotation of despotism with which the word has been associated ever since the classical Greeks forged the close connexion. This will become very clear when we turn, in Chapter 10, to the Peisistratids in Athens. Not that the descendants of the first autocrats, in their efforts to maintain dynastic rule, did not customarily become brutal despots and get themselves thrown out—Archaic tyrannies were all short-lived in terms of generations—but the rise of the individual tyrannies and their role were rooted in the whole social situation, not simply in the moral quality of certain individuals.

Beginning probably after the middle of the seventh century, tyranny spread to many communities of mainland Greece and later to the Aegean islands, to Asia

Minor and to the western communities. Our chief source of information is Herodotus, who does not pretend to have an exact chronology, and the efforts in this direction by later Greek antiquarians and historians are unreliable, so that it is safer not to give precise dates in most instances. The earliest and in some ways most ambiguous of the tyrants was Pheidon of Argos, described by Aristotle (*Politics* 1310b26–8) as a king who rules as a tyrant, a pointed formulation suggesting that Pheidon was a genuine autocrat, unlike the hereditary kings before him; perhaps the introduction of the phalanx was his way of solidifying his power over the other nobles. Within a generation or so, more typical tyrannies appeared in Corinth, Sicyon and Megara, to cite the best known. That roster, as well as the sixth-century instances of Athens, Naxos, Samos or Miletus, all point to a high (though not perfect) correlation between tyranny on the one hand and more advanced economic and political development, in particular urbanism, on the other. Hence the most backward regions, such as Acarnania, Aetolia or Thessaly, rarely enter into consideration.

The common factor was the inability of the hereditary aristocracies to contain or resolve the growing conflicts, whether those within their own ranks or those involving the wealthier commoners, the growing urban population, and the debt-ridden and impoverished peasantry. Conflicts with other states were sometimes a further factor, as in Argos against Sparta or in Athens against Megara. It is no accident that in the 'colonial' areas the appearance of tyranny was later by a century and more, and then was often meshed in with the problems created by powerful neighbouring states, Lydia or Persia in the east, Carthage in the west. Polycrates of Samos benefited greatly by the need to organize resistance to Persia on an unprecedented scale and by his ability to achieve that. Others, in contrast, based their less spectacular tyrannies on Persian support.

Thus there was a military side to tyranny, but the bodyguards and troops, whether native or mercenary, must not be allowed to conceal its very considerable popularity. In every city there were elements who *wanted* a tyrant, expecting him to achieve by threats and force the social and political aims they felt incapable of achieving otherwise. In Athens there had been an unsuccessful coup by a man named Cylon about 630 B.C. A generation later there was a popular demand that Solon become a tyrant, on the model of the tyrannies of neighbouring Megara and Corinth. Solon refused—a rare and notable self-denial—and tried to bring about reform by other means, but the significant fact remains that there was a serious demand. And in many places tyranny did accomplish, at the expense of the traditional aristocracy, precisely what was asked of it. This is not to suggest that the tyrants saw themselves as the bearers of some mysterious historic destiny or as the forerunners of democracy or of anything else. They wanted power and success, and if they were intelligent and disciplined, they gained it for themselves by advancing their communities. They put an end, for a generation or two, to crippling *stasis*; they entered into alliances, by dynastic marriages and other devices, with other Greek states and were thus a force for peace where that was possible (as it sometimes was not); they nurtured peasant independence and perhaps fostered trade and manufacture (though this is far from clear in the available evidence); they strengthened the sense of community by public works and splendid festivals, focused largely around major cults. Above all, they broke the habit of old-fashioned aristocratic rule. The paradox is that, standing above the law and above the constitution, the tyrants in the end strengthened the *polis* and its institutions and helped raise the *demos*, the people as a whole, to a level of political self-consciousness which then led, in some states, to government by the *demos*, democracy.

The great weakness of tyranny was, of course, that its operations and tone depended so heavily on the personal qualities of the tyrant. Another was its seductiveness. The tyrant was not the only able and ambitious man in his state, but there was no place for the others commensurate with their claims, and there was no form which political rivalry could take other than conspiracy and assassination. Hence tyranny led structurally, usually in the second generation or at the latest in the third, to despotism, civil war and either abdication or overthrow. What followed differed from community to community. The centuries of uneven development in the Greek world had left a permanent legacy of considerable variation. Two states emerged as the most important, each in its way exceptional: Sparta, which avoided tyranny altogether, and Athens, which was to become the paragon of Greek democracy and also Greece's most important imperial power.

9

Sparta

NOT the least unusual feature of Sparta was the peculiar relationship between *polis* and territory: the *polis* of Sparta consisted, at least ideally, of a single class of 'Equals' or 'Peers' (*homoioi*) residing in the centre and ruling over a relatively vast subject population. Sparta was located on the right bank of the Eurotas River, in a broken plain of nearly 700 square miles, the heart of the district of Laconia. After she conquered Messenia, her total territory amounted to some 3200 square miles, more than three times as large as Attica. Given the nature of Greek terrain, this figure is not very meaningful. What is crucial is that Messenia and, to a lesser extent, Laconia were more fertile than most Greek districts, so that the inhabitants were able to feed themselves without imports, except perhaps when there was heavy and prolonged fighting. Laconia also possessed iron mines, a great rarity in Greece, though it must be admitted that we do not know how early they were worked. The main weakness was poor access to the sea. Sparta herself was, strictly speaking, landlocked: the nearest available harbour was Gytheion some twenty-seven miles to the south, used both for merchant shipping and as a small naval base.

The Spartans themselves were not a very numerous group. The largest military contingent they ever mustered from their own ranks was at the battle against the Persians at Plataea in 479 B.C.—5000 hoplites. With them and serving in their army on that occasion were 5000 *perioeci*, men from the rest of Laconia (and perhaps a few from Messenia), who were free men living in their own small communities (such as Gytheion) but differing from the normal Greek pattern in that they lacked autonomy in the military sphere and in foreign affairs generally. In those respects they were subject to Sparta, obligated to accept Spartan policy and to fight in the Spartan army at the latter's call and under Spartan authority. Although subjects and not to be confused with genuine allies, such as the Corinthians, the *perioeci* were at the same time citizens of their own communities, Doric in their dialect and entitled like the Spartans themselves to be called Lacedaemonians, after their eponymous ancestor, Lacedaemon, son of Zeus and Taygete (nymph of nearby Mt. Taygetus). They were thus sharply differentiated from the remaining and most numerous subject population, the helots.

The origin of the helot system has been the topic of endless unconvincing speculation ever since antiquity. There were parallels elsewhere in the Greek world, in Crete, in Thessaly and in the colonized regions both east and west, but even less is known about them, so that they do not help solve the helot mystery. The usual practice, throughout most of antiquity, when a city or district was enslaved, was to sell off the inhabitants and disperse them. In Laconia, however, the Spartans adopted the dangerous alternative of keeping a whole population in subjugation at home, in what amounted to their native territory, and later (probably in the eighth century) they repeated the pattern when they conquered Messenia.

In that they lacked personal freedom, the helots were slaves, but they must be differentiated in several respects from the genuine slaves, who were chattels, the personal property of their masters. The helots were subjects of the Spartan state assigned to individuals, not free to move or to control their own lives, but possessing certain rights, which were normally honoured. Their basic obligation was to work the land and attend to the pastures of the Spartans to whom they were bound, and to pay over half the produce. They maintained their own family relationships and for the large part they lived in their own cohesive groups ('communities' would be too strong a word). Hence they were self-perpetuating: we never hear of Sparta importing new helots from abroad, and that fact alone sets them sharply apart from the chattel slaves elsewhere.

Whatever the origins of the system—how, for example, an original distinction was drawn in Laconia between the two very different subject statuses, *perioeci* and helots, or how the helots came to be monopolized by the Spartans and not also assigned to *perioeci*, who were in turn free to obtain and own genuine slaves if they wished—the consequences in historical times are intelligible enough. As we shall see, the helots, proportionally far more numerous than the slaves of any other Greek state, even Athens, were fundamental to the establishment of the unique Spartan system, and to the policies adopted by Sparta abroad.

Our ignorance of Dark Age Sparta extends still further, to the whole of its early institutional development. Archaeology has been even less helpful than usual here. The only prudent course, therefore, is to turn immediately to the Archaic period, from the early seventh century, putting aside all the efforts to reconstruct something coherent out of the blatant fictions permeating later traditions, including those which eventually become attached to the legendary lawgiver Lycurgus. Not that our evidence for seventh-century Sparta is abundant, but it at least has a firm anchor; some of it is contemporary and is subject to the normal controls of historical analysis. We can, for example, read the fragments of the lyric poet Alcman, which immediately suggests that Sparta in his time was still within the mainstream of Greek cultural development, as it later was not. Other signs point in the same direction, such as the archaeological finds or the plausible tradition about Sparta's leading role in the development of Greek music (whether or not one chooses to believe that it was a Lydian named Terpander, the inventor of the lyre, who migrated to Sparta and founded the musical tradition there). We can read the fragments of the poet Tyrtaeus, which reveal that seventh-century Sparta was also within the mainstream in its condition of chronic *stasis* (again as it later was not), involving struggles over land distribution, political demands by commoners (with the new hoplite army an important factor), and conflicts with other states in the Peloponnese, notably with Argos and with Tegea, the leading city in Arcadia.

There is even a curious story about a colony Sparta sent out to Taras (modern Taranto) in southern Italy about 700 B.C. Actually, there are two versions, each with variants, which were bitterly debated in antiquity. According to one (Strabo VI 3, 2), those Spartiates who had not participated in the conquest of Messenia, which took many years, were afterwards enslaved by the returning warriors, while 'children born during the war were called Partheniae [from the word *parthenos* meaning both "virgin" and "unmarried woman"] and deprived of civic rights. The Partheniae, being numerous, refused to accept their lot and conspired against the *demos*.' The plot was discovered, the Delphic oracle advised shipping them out to Taras, and there they joined with the barbarians and Cretans who were already settled on the site. In the alternative account, also recorded by Strabo (VI 3, 3), the Spartan women sent a delegation to the army after the war had dragged on for ten years, protesting the depopulation that was the inevitable consequence. The best young men were sent home to procreate, but when the full army finally returned, they failed to 'honour the Partheniae as the others but treated them as illegitimate. The latter thereupon conspired with some of the helots and revolted'; the plot was revealed by helots, and again the foundation of Taras was the final outcome.

Apart from Taras—and Spartan participation in its settlement is certain however one threads one's way through the conflicting tales—Sparta was never involved in the Archaic colonization movement. The reason lies in her extensive territory, especially after the conquest of Messenia, and this factor together with the system of *perioeci* and helots constituted a fundamental breach in the 'typical' Greek pattern of development. In the end Sparta had no choice but to take a road essentially different from that of any other state. The turning-point came in the so-called Second Messenian War, which, the tradition says, lasted seventeen years, and which is probably to be dated in the third quarter of the seventh century. Messenia revolted and the Spartans found themselves very hard pressed to put down the uprising, primarily, it would seem from Tyrtaeus, because of disaffection, disorder and near-rebellion in their own ranks.

During this struggle Tyrtaeus called for *eunomia*, 'obedience to the laws', which was to become, in the eyes of some Greeks, Sparta's greatest virtue in classical times. (It is worth noticing that in all his exhortations to patriotism and *eunomia*, Tyrtaeus never mentioned the lawgiver Lycurgus.) And once the Messenians were subjugated again, the Spartans proceeded to work out a common solution to their two most pressing problems, the elimination of *stasis* at home and the maintenance of a secure hold on the helots who greatly outnumbered the free men. We cannot trace the precise steps through which the solution—a compromise among various conflicting groups and demands—was finally achieved (and there were further changes in the following centuries within the framework of that compromise). There is no agreement among scholars, for example, as to the date or precise significance of a key document, the so-called Great Rhetra, preserved by Plutarch (*Life of Lycurgus* VI) in corrupt wording within a confused context. On any interpretation, that brief text, which distributes the power of decision-making among the kings, the council of elders, and the assembly of all the equals, marks the first time in Greek history that the popular assembly was assigned formal, though restricted, powers, at a date which is probably earlier than the Second Messenian War. (The Rhetra makes no reference to the ephors, who were already in existence and who later, by the middle of the sixth century, became the most important executive authority in the Spartan government.) The measure of both our ignorance and the amount of development in Spartan institutions which must be allowed for, is thus sufficiently exemplified in this single text.

Eunomia was achieved, according to Herodotus (I 65), in the reign of Kings Leon and Agasicles, that is, early in the sixth century. 'Before then,' he writes, 'they were the worst ruled of nearly all the Greeks, both in their internal relations and in their relations with foreigners, from whom they were isolated.' If this has any foundation, it means that the two generations after the Second Messenian War saw the working out of the rather complex structure of historical Spartan society. The male Spartiates, the Equals, were now a full-time military establishment. Their lives were, in principle, wholly moulded by, and wholly dedicated to, the state. Even the decision whether or not a male infant should be allowed to survive was taken away from the parents and handed over to public officials. This was one of many devices which served, both symbolically and in practice, to minimize the bonds of kinship and thereby to reduce a major source of conflicting loyalties. At seven a boy was turned over to the state for his education, with its concentration on physical hardihood, military skills and the virtues of obedience. In childhood and adolescence he progressed through a series of intimate age-class groupings; as an adult his main association was with his military regiment and his mess-hall. Various rituals reinforced the system at fixed stages in a man's growth.

Concentration on the single purpose of the Spartiate's life was strengthened by his release from all economic concerns and activities. That was the responsibility of the helots and the *perioeci*, who, in their different ways, produced the food and armour and carried on the necessary trade. The helots worked under absolute compulsion, of course, but the *perioeci* were the beneficiaries of a monopolistic position, free from competition either from Spartans themselves or from outsiders. Spartiates were even prohibited from employing coined money, and outsiders were denied all access to the economy except through the mediation of the *perioeci* or the state. This probably helps to explain why we hear little of unrest on the part of the *perioeci*, despite their lack of autonomy and their obligatory military contribution. It also explains the failure of Sparta to grow into an urban community. 'If Sparta were to be deserted,' wrote Thucydides (I 10, 2), 'and only the sanctuaries and building foundations remained, future generations would never believe that her power matched her reputation ... for they live in villages according to the old Greek fashion.'

From childhood, too, the Spartiates were encouraged in competition among each other, not in intellectual achievement or for economic advantage but in physical prowess and stamina. The prizes were honorific rather than material in one sense, but among them were positions of authority and leadership. Already at the age of eighteen one might be rewarded by admission to the élite youth corps called *hippeis*, whose functions included serving as the royal bodyguard and carrying out secret governmental missions. Then came the chance for army commands and eventually government posts.

At the head of the governmental structure stood the two hereditary kings, an anomalous institution which is not easy to define (and the co-existence of two royal houses has defied explanation). They commanded the armies in the field. At home, however, they not only lacked authoritative royal powers but they were subject to supervision by the ephors. On the other hand, they retained certain traditional priestly functions; they received by right various perquisites; and on their death they were mourned on a scale and in a manner which Herodotus (VI 58) found so alien that he called the royal funeral rites 'similar to those of the barbarians of Asia'. They were *ex officio* members of the *gerousia*, a council of thirty elders, the others being men over the age of sixty elected for life. The kings seem not to have presided over the *gerousia* nor to have had any prerogatives in its deliberations beyond those of any other member. Nor did they preside over meetings of the assembly, which apparently could not initiate action or even amend proposals brought before it, but which nevertheless had the final vote in basic questions of policy submitted to it. And then there were the five ephors, elected annually from among the whole citizen-body and restricted to a single year in office, during which they had far-reaching powers in criminal jurisdiction and general administration.

The very existence of the two royal houses is one indication that the ideal of a community of Equals was incomplete in reality. The constitution may have hemmed the kings in, but the aura surrounding them encouraged and assisted the abler and more ambitious of them to extend their authority in a way that sometimes endangered the power equilibrium of the society. Herodotus is almost obsessed with stories about the susceptibility of Spartan kings to bribery. When Aristagoras, tyrant of Miletus, seeking Spartan support for the Ionian revolt against Persia, had raised his offer to Cleomenes I from ten to fifty talents, the king was saved from temptation only because his eight- or nine-year-old daughter Gorgo cried out, 'Father, the foreigner will ruin you if you do not withdraw' (V 51). Some ephors, too, found the extensive authority given to them very heady wine, which they sought to taste to the full in the one year of office allowed them. It often happened, according to Aristotle (*Politics* 1270b7–15.), 'that very poor men attained this office, whose lack of means enabled them to be bought'; yet, such was their power, that even the kings 'were compelled to court them'.

All this may be grossly exaggerated (or, in Aristotle's case, it may refer to Sparta in its decline in the fourth century) but it nevertheless reveals that Spartan austerity was never as complete in reality as on paper. Besides there was inequality in wealth among the Equals. Some were even rich enough to enter teams in the Olympic chariot races, the paramount sign of outstanding wealth among aristocratic Greeks; surviving records list the names of nine Spartan winners (with twelve victories among them) between 550 and 400 B.C., one of them a king, Damaratus; another, Arcesilaus, twice a victor, was followed by his son twenty years later. Did men of such wealth never use it to advance their own interests in elections or those of their sons all along the line? That would be hard to imagine, just as it is difficult to appreciate the overtones of a meeting of the Spartan assembly, which was not heterogeneous like the Athenian but rather a meeting, in another capacity, of a highly disciplined army corps for whom obedience had been held up as the prime virtue all their lives. Could they have listened to debates with an open mind, disregarding the status of the speakers in the army hierarchy or their individual exploits on the battlefield?

Answers to such questions must be speculative because our ancient authorities are not concerned with them. Internal conflicts appear in the historical record we have, at least for the sixth century, only in accounts of the more spectacular careers of a few individuals, and then almost entirely in the context of foreign affairs. Herodotus will pause to tell (V 39–40) how first the ephors and then the elders brought pressure on the childless King Anaxandridas to take another wife in order to preserve his royal line, threatening him with some unspecified action by the Spartans as a whole should he persist in his obstinate refusal. But conflicts over broader issues or over control of affairs and something of the actual mechanics of policy-making do not really come to light until a man like Cleomenes I, king from about 520 to 490, employed his military successes and his diplomatic manœuvres to direct Spartan policy towards aggressive and dangerous adventures abroad.

It was accepted by ancient writers that the key to Spartan foreign policy was the presence of the helots. To hold them in check, Sparta had not only to keep peace in the Peloponnese, for an enemy state might stir up the helots, if not by design then by the mere fact of engaging too much of Spartan military energies and manpower, but she also had to be very careful before sending an army outside the Peloponnese. Spartan policy had not always been defensive and non-expansionist. But a defeat by Tegea and the inability to conquer Argos seem finally to have initiated the new policy by the middle of the sixth century. Wars and conquests were replaced by defensive alliances and non-aggression pacts, though naturally force was used to impose alliances when necessary and also to maintain them against defections. By the end of the century, virtually the whole of the Peloponnese had been brought into the network, except Argos which was too strong and Achaea which was too remote and insignificant. To strengthen the alliances, furthermore, Sparta supported friendly factions within the allied states, normally oligarchies, and in the process she gained the undeserved reputation of being the sworn enemy of tyrants on principle. In fact, Spartan behaviour towards tyrants was opportunistic, determined by judgments of self-interest rather than of morals and principles. She never moved against the tyrannies of Corinth or Megara, for example, whereas she interfered decisively to bring about the expulsion of Hippias from Athens in 510.[1]

The Athenian adventure is reported in our sources as part of the story of Cleomenes I, with the stress on the king himself. Perhaps he was the chief advocate or even the initiator of the policy, but there can be little doubt that he marched on Athens in his official capacity and with official sanction. Then came complications as two factions in Athens engaged in a civil war over the succession to the tyranny. Cleomenes returned to support one faction, led by Isagoras, against that of Cleisthenes. He suffered a defeat, left Athens and returned once again with an army enlarged by allied troops. When the latter learned why they had been mustered, they rebelled, under the leadership of Corinth, saying that intervention in Athenian domestic affairs was unjust and anyway no business of theirs. The other Spartan king, Damaratus, supported them, and the whole venture ended in a fiasco for Cleomenes, with important consequences.

Henceforth the allies were consulted, in more or less formal meetings called for the purpose, whenever their military support was wanted, or at least when a large-scale joint operation was envisaged. A loose network of alliances between Sparta on the one hand and each of her allies individually on the other, was now converted into something approaching a genuine league. Modern historians actually call it the Peloponnesian League, though the Greeks always clung to 'the Spartans and their allies' and though its membership at various times included such states outside the Peloponnese as Megara, Aegina and Athens. In a sense the modern name goes too far: the 'league' never acquired any administrative machinery, not even a treasury, and its cohesion and effectiveness varied from decade to decade, and from issue to issue. Nevertheless, it was enough of a reality to give Sparta the added manpower she needed, and the peace at home, to become the greatest military force in Greece and the acknowledged leader of the Greeks against the Persian invaders.

[1] For the Athenian side of this episode, see the final pages of the next chapter.

10

Athens

GEOGRAPHICALLY the district of Attica, some 1000 square miles in all, is typically Greek, not so fertile as the best, such as Messenia, but with a number of good extensive plains nonetheless. Two features require special mention. Attica had a very considerable coast-line on the south and east suitable for beaching ships, and in the southeast, at Laurium, there was a rich supply of silver, which had been tapped as early as the Bronze Age and was mined in the Archaic age from the ninth century. But there was nothing in the terrain to promote the early and exceptional political unification of the district. Nor is the ethnic argument a sufficient explanation: neighbouring Boeotia remained politically fragmented, after all.

Not only was Athens the largest Greek city-state territorially, apart from Sparta, but, unlike the latter, she became a unified state without internal subjects, not even *perioeci*, let alone helots. All free men of Attica were equally Athenians, whether they lived in the main city or in Marathon or Eleusis or elsewhere in the countryside. The sharp class inequalities that existed were based neither on region nor on ethnic distinctions, but were repeated throughout the various demes or districts of the state; the slaves came from outside. To be sure, the size of the state meant that such larger 'villages' as Marathon had a semi-independent life of their own, with their own agoras, village officials, temples and cults. This regionalism, as some modern scholars refer to it, should not be exaggerated; in particular, it must be wholly differentiated from the more typical situation in Boeotia already noticed, with its twelve independent, and often quarrelling, city-states. The Athenians were themselves well aware that they were an exception in this respect, and in characteristic fashion they attributed the unification of Attica, or *synoikismos* as they called it, to a single heroic figure, King Theseus whom we have met before. That this is a mythical explanation (probably of the sixth century) is implicit in the vague and anachronistic account of the *synoikismos* given by Thucydides (II 15–16). Once Theseus, a sort of latter-day Heracles, is removed, there is no evidence that Attica was ever anything but a unit (though we must allow for possible disputes over such a border district as Eleusis), with a political development in the Bronze and Dark Ages—Mycenaean monarchy, breakdown, Dark Age chieftainship and finally aristocratic rule—that followed the lines already described for other Greek states, apart from the one aberration of size, for which no better explanation than the mythical one is available.[1]

Athens also took no part in the colonization movement. Though individual Athenians may have migrated, the city as such, unlike Sparta, had not even one Taras to her credit. Perhaps her large territory provided an outlet which other states had to find abroad. Besides, her continuous record of pottery production, from the earliest protogeometric, implies a better than average industrial development, which may have acted as a second safety valve against rural depression and overpopulation. In the end, however, Athens could not escape the universal *stasis* of archaic Greece, with the same issues, the same conflicting social groupings, the same call for a tyrant. The economic and political monopoly of the Eupatrid families (as the Athenian aristocracy were called, the word meaning 'well-sired') was menaced, both from within the closed circle and from the lower classes, in the second half of the seventh century, when the crisis appears to have arisen with some suddenness.

The first recorded episode was an unsuccessful attempt to establish tyranny in about 630 by a nobleman named Cylon. Later Athenian accounts pretend that Cylon drew his support mainly from outside, in particular from his father-in-law Theagenes, tyrant of Megara; that the Athe-

---

[1] This reduction of the *synoikismos* of Theseus to a complete myth is not the view generally accepted by historians. It is based on the investigations of J. Sarkady, published in German in the *Acta classica* of the University of Debrecen, vol. 2 (1966), pp. 9–27; vol. 3 (1967). pp. 23–34.

nians resisted *en masse*; and that the Eupatrid house of the
Alcmaeonids brought a curse upon themselves by violat-
ing a safe-conduct and massacring Cylon's followers. The
distortion seems fairly obvious. Tyrants everywhere had
considerable internal support; even the Athenians had no
choice but to admit that a generation later there was a
popular demand for Solon to assume the role of tyrant. On
the other hand, there is no inherent improbability in the
family connexion between Cylon and Theagenes: such
marriages were an essential part of inter-city relations and
few aristocratic families had any reluctance in accepting a
tyrant as son-in-law or father-in-law. As for the massacre
following Cylon's surrender, there may have been a mur-
derous vendetta for some years, which would explain the
shadowy figure of Draco. He is supposed to have codified
the law in 621 — 'a code written in blood, not in ink', a later
hostile tradition said of it (Plutarch, *Solon* XVII 2), a tradition remarkably free from concrete data. What Draco
probably did do was to lay down in detail the law regarding
murder. Some of that law was still in force at the end of the
fifth century B.C., and the little we know deals primarily
with ways of putting an end to the traditional blood-feud.
This is what the post-Cylonian blood-letting may have
been responsible for. A total codification by Draco, however, is quite certainly fictitious. That was the work of
Solon in the next generation.

With Solon we possess a body of genuine documentation
for the first time, small though it is. He was himself a fairly
prolific writer on ethical and political themes. Like all
writers in this age of minimal literacy, he expressed himself
not in prose but in poems, which survived for centuries. A
few extensive quotations are still available. Besides, the
original text of his law code, inscribed on wooden tablets,
remained in existence for many years, though the con-
fusion in the sources has led to disagreement among
modern scholars about the details, even about how long
they continued to be accessible.

Solon was a Eupatrid who in 594 was appointed archon,
the highest office in the state, with plenipotentiary powers
to put an end to the *stasis* by a thoroughgoing reform of the

laws and the political system. Both the choice of Solon and the way it was made are significant. He did not seize power but was appointed to it, which proves that among the aristocracy itself a sufficient number were ready to accept major concessions to the clamouring opposition, many of them peasants in bondage and clientship (as explained in Chapter 8). The only hope for a successful compromise lay with an aristocrat who had taken his stand with the poor. Solon, we know from his earlier poems, had placed the onus for bringing the state to civil war on the rapacity and inhumanity of the rich. And he seems to have done so by public recitation, in the agora.

> Unrighteous are the hearts of the rulers of the people, who will one day suffer many pains for their great pride (*hybris*); for they do not know how to restrain their excesses.... They grow rich through unrighteous deeds, and steal for themselves right and left, respecting neither sacred not public property....
>
> (quoted by Demosthenes XIX 255)

The poor repaid him by an appeal that he become tyrant. This he refused, but he accepted the extraordinary archonship and proceeded to steer a complicated course between the extreme demands of the peasantry and the hard-bitten wing of the nobility.

His first action, the so-called *seisachtheia* or 'shaking off of burdens', was directed to the fundamental question of peasant bondage. Debts were cancelled, the many Athenians who were tied down as involuntary share-croppers (*hektemoroi*) or who had been taken into bondage as a result of indebtedness were restored to freedom, others who had actually been sold abroad into slavery were bought back. A new law was then promulgated forbidding for all future time the practice of mortgaging the persons of free men or women as security for debts. Solon refused, however, to take the most revolutionary step of all, confiscation of large estates for distribution among the poorest peasants and the landless. Nevertheless, Aristotle (*Constitution of Athens* IX 1) was right to put the *seisachtheia* first among the Solonic measures in the interest of the common people. A free peasantry was to be the base of Athenian society all through her history as an independent *polis*. Serious weaknesses still remained in their position, but they were henceforth protected from the traditional forms of personal exploitation, a protection which Solon further strengthened by reforms in the administration of justice and by his codification of the law, an action which introduced clarity, certainty and public knowledge of the law into the community.

On the constitutional side the balance required was more complex, for in that sphere there were conflicts within the upper classes themselves. Solon's most decisive thrust was the creation of a formal status hierarchy based on wealth as the sole criterion. The citizen-body was divided into four classes according to wealth, measured, it is essential to stress, not in money but in agricultural yield. The highest offices, with a one-year tenure, were restricted to the first class, men whose land produced 500 dry or liquid measures.[1] One of these offices, the archonship, was the way of entry into the Council of the Areopagus, the traditional body of life peers with a general undefined supervisory authority over the state (reminiscent of the Roman Senate), which Solon retained. The next two classes were eligible for the minor offices and presumably for the new council of 400 which Solon created. The rest, the *thetes*, those who could not produce 200 measures a year, were restricted to the assembly.

Just how the assembly or the council of 400 functioned in the spheres of legislation and policy is the subject of much speculation. The sources have little to relate, apart from one very important new feature, namely, the grant to the assembly of apellate jurisdiction over the magistrates in some lawsuits. But the thinking behind the reforms and their general impact are clear. The wealthiest commoners became eligible for the highest offices and the Areopagus,

---

[1] The dry measure was the *medimnos* (just under 1½ bushels), the liquid measure the *metretes* (about 8½ imperial gallons). The arbitrary attribution of equality in value to the two measures, like the failure to differentiate between one crop and another, or between wine and oil, reveals how far the economy was from a market-and-money system of evaluation.

thus breaking the Eupatrid monopoly though by no means removing the latter from power and influence, since they no doubt still constituted a majority of the largest land-owners. The middle classes, including the hoplite soldiers who held sufficient land, were given a role in government for the first time. And even the poor, both urban and rural, were recognized as a working part of the *demos* as a whole, severely restricted though their position was. The great gaps in the structure of the rudimentary *polis*, which had prevented it from functioning as a viable community, were thus narrowed, though they were not yet sealed off.

Solon then left Athens for a long period, fearing that, if he remained, the dissatisfied extremists would put pressure on him to make further changes or to go on to become a tyrant. Factional disturbances continued. On two occasions it proved impossible to choose an archon. We hear no more of this kind of trouble after 580 B.C., presumably because the new constitutional machinery became formally accepted by most of the wealthier classes, Eupatrid and commoner alike. However, constitutional machinery alone could not give internal peace. *Stasis* could not be abolished by a stroke of the pen. The personal status of the peasantry had been secured by Solon, but not their economic position. Nor, apparently, could the city provide a livelihood for enough of the landless and the others who were unable to make ends meet in the countryside. Demands and counter-demands played into the hands of the more ambitious of the aristocrats able to draw upon retainers and followers in the continual jockeying for honour, power and wealth. Eventually one man rose above them all and achieved what Solon had tried to prevent. Peisistratus, an influential aristocrat who claimed a family tree going back to Homer's Nestor and who had gained public repute in a war with Megara, made his first attempt, according to the tradition, in 561. He was expelled after a time, tried again, was again expelled, and finally succeeded in 545. He then ruled until his death in 527 and was followed by his son Hippias, whose tyranny was not brought to an end until 510, and then only thanks to an invading Spartan army (Chapter 9).

There is no contemporary literary evidence about the Peisistratids. Our first account of them is that of Herodotus, writing in the middle of the next century, when every right-thinking Greek automatically condemned tyranny and all tyrants as an unmitigated evil. It is all the more revealing, therefore, that Herodotus and serious later writers were agreed that Peisistratus was an exception, a 'good tyrant' insofar as that phrase was not self-contradictory. 'He governed the city with moderation, as citizen rather than as tyrant' (Aristotle, *Constitution of Athens* XVI 2). They also agreed that one secret of his success, and of his son's, was that they left Solon's constitution in operation unchanged, except that they saw to it that the annually elected archon was always either a member of the family or a supporter. We should not understand this in a naïve way, though the statement is undoubtedly correct as bare fact. Peisistratus' first attempt or attempts to seize power (it is not certain that the tradition is right about two failures) seem to have been made with such support as he could muster within Attica. But the third time, equipped with funds he acquired from the silver mines of Mt. Pangaeum in Thrace, he came with a mercenary force, some of whom he retained as a bodyguard in his citadel on the Acropolis. His irreconcilable opponents were killed or exiled. Thus protected, Peisistratus could afford to allow the machinery of assembly, council, magistrates and courts, even the Council of the Areopagus, to go on functioning. On the other hand, no one could compel him to rule 'constitutionally'. That he did so from choice is a measure of his political intelligence, and in the end it is one key to his place in the evolution of the Athenian state.

The precise relationship between the Peisistratids and the other aristocratic families of Athens during their thirty-five-year period in power is not easy to define. Later traditions of the undying enmity of such families as the Alcmaeonids may be discounted as *post factum* attempts to purge the family records of their friendly associations with the departed tyranny. The Alcmaeonids did make an unsuccessful attempt to overthrow Hippias in 513, but, before that, one of them, Cleisthenes, had held the archonship under Hippias, and still earlier his sister had been married to Peisistratus. Relations were equally ambiguous and shifting between the Peisistratids and the Miltiades family. The latter were connected by marriage with the Cypselids, tyrants of Corinth, while Cleisthenes' mother was the daughter of the tyrant of Sicyon, in accord with the practice we have already noted in connexion with Cylon in the seventh century. Another of Peisistratus' wives was an Argive aristocrat who had previously been married to a tyrant in Ambracia, a member of the Cypselid clan. Other connexions of the Peisistratids are recorded in Euboea, in Thrace and Macedonia, in Thessaly and with Lygdamis, tyrant of Naxos. Aristotle's generalization, in his *Constitution of Athens* (XVI 9), that Peisistratus won the support of the majority of the nobility and the people alike, may thus be extended, so far as the nobility were concerned, to connexions abroad.

Much as the Greek aristocracy of the time may have preferred oligarchy to rule by one man from their ranks, they rarely carried their preference to a point of principle. Disputes between a tyrant and an aristocratic individual or family were generated primarily by considerations of personal honour or status. Even the assassination of Hippias' younger brother Hipparchus in 514, which led to the hardening of the tyranny into a more despotic rule, was motivated by jealousy in a pederastic love affair. The Athenians subsequently made national heroes of the two assassins, Harmodius and Aristogeiton, but that reflects public opinion in the age when the tyranny had been judged infamous in retrospect.

However, the Athenian aristocracy suffered a permanent defeat under the Peisistratids. Thirty-five years of the Solonic constitution at work, even with the tyrant as permanent overseer, could not be undone, especially when the period was also one of peace and growing prosperity for Athens. The leading families still held the main offices and still involved themselves in foreign relations, but they were also being tamed in the process, compelled and increasingly accustomed to function within a constitutional framework, in which the previous factional activities were curbed. When Hippias was driven into exile by the Spartans in 510, one wing of the aristocracy, led by Isagoras, sought to return to the good old days. They were defeated in a two-year civil war, after which Cleisthenes remodelled the constitution and laid the structural foundation of Athenian democracy. In this he was no doubt much aided by a 'national' spirit to which the tyrants had contributed actively and concretely. They built a great temple to Athena on the Acropolis (destroyed by the Persians in 480 and later replaced by the Parthenon) and began one to Olympian Zeus; they encouraged and embellished the major cults, introducing recitations from Homer into the Panathenaic festival which celebrated the birth of Athena, and the annual competition in tragic choruses at the Greater Dionysia; they patronized the arts generally and invited poets and musicians from abroad to their court in Athens.

The impact of these cultural factors cannot be overlooked even if it cannot be measured (and it is not lessened by acknowledging that the tyrants' interest was in their own glory as much as, or more than, in fostering a national self-consciousness). Part of the impact was on the economy. Athens was still a largely agrarian community and the prime test of economic stability was in the countryside. We know little about Peisistratean activity there, other than the support they gave to needy farmers by making loans available on easy terms, but all the evidence of the next century goes to show that the tyranny was the period when the class of owners of small and medium-sized farms became firmly and permanently entrenched. This would have been harder, if not impossible, to achieve, had there not been a considerable growth in the urban sector of the economy, providing an outlet for landless and marginal peasants, among other things.

The great attention to public buildings and festivals was one factor in the growth of the city economy. So was the remarkable upsurge in Athenian fine painted pottery, which about the middle of the sixth century rapidly acquired a virtual monopoly among Greek pottery exports to the other cities of Greece, to the western colonies, and to the Etruscans. Athenian coinage is still another sign:

although it is not certain exactly when Athens began to mint silver, the decisive shift to the famous 'owls', the one genuinely international Greek currency, occurred either in Peisistratus' reign or in his son's. And, finally, more and more Greeks began to migrate to Athens from other cities, as new prospects were opened up for trade and manufacture, and as she blossomed into a pan-Hellenic cultural centre.

Later Athenians looked back to Solon as the man who set them on the road to democracy, whereas Peisistratus and Hippias were an uncomfortable and not very reputable interlude. Nevertheless, if we put aside moral judgments and considerations of intention or foresight, the historical role of the tyrants appears to have been equally important in moving the Athenians along the road.

11

The Culture of Archaic Greece

FOR all their geographical dispersion and their political fragmentation, the Greeks retained a deep-rooted consciousness of belonging to a single and unique culture—'being of the same stock and the same speech, with common shrines of the gods and rituals, with similar customs', as Herodotus (VIII 144) phrased it. They were right—and the phenomenon is remarkable, given the absence of a central political or ecclesiastical authority, the predominantly oral character of their culture even beyond the end of the Archaic period, and the inventiveness with which one community or another solved problem after problem in politics and culture. Perhaps nothing is so revealing as the rapidity with which a new idea was diffused. The Phoenician alphabet is an early example; others are the council-magistrate-assembly machinery of government, the 'Doric' temple and coined money. It seems not to have mattered whether an 'invention' was Greek to begin with or borrowed from outside. If it proved functional within Greek society in general and compatible with local conditions, then its value was quickly recognized in practice all over the Greek world.

One binding element was myth. The Greeks had a large stock of mythical tales. There was a myth behind every rite and every cult-centre, behind new city-foundations, and for more or less everything in nature, the movement of the sun, the stars, rivers and springs, earthquakes and plagues. Myth performed a number of functions: it was explanatory, didactic and prescriptive. It gave the archaic Greeks their sense of, and knowledge of, their past, their history in other words; it sanctioned cults, festivals, beliefs, the authority of individual noble families (with their divine genealogies), and so on through a range of practices and ideas. On the other hand, myth was not all-controlling. As we saw in discussing the lawgivers in Chapter 8, there was also much human self-reliance behind the evolution of institutions and ideas, a readiness to change and innovate without direct divine authority or revelation. Increasingly, the Greeks found themselves with separate, sometimes irreconcilable, mythical and non-mythical explanations and justifications, co-existing happily. The myths were believed to be true, though there was neither a sanctified priesthood nor any other pre-ordained authority with the prerogative to develop new myths or to certify old ones. From the sixth century B.C. on, an occasional voice was raised in doubt or scepticism; not many, however, for most people did not *study* the myths, they merely retold them or they performed the appropriate rites and that was sufficient.

The mythmaking process continued. Thus, as the Greeks dispersed east and west, Apollo, Demeter, Heracles and the other gods and demi-gods had to travel with them, and the myths were adjusted and enlarged accordingly. The Greeks in Sicily challenged the claim of Eleusis to be the place where Demeter, goddess of the fertility of the earth, first gave man the gift of corn. Heracles swam the Straits of Messina and then took a grand tour of Sicily which brought him as far as Eryx in the northwest, thereby sanctioning Greek claims to that part of the island. Aphrodite followed later, and it was from Eryx that her cult spread to Carthage and to Rome. In Old Greece, too, myths had to support shifting political relations and alliances, ideas of 'ethnic' cohesion (as with the Ionians), or the conflicting claims of certain shrines to higher status than others. The longest of the so-called 'Homeric Hymns' is about Apollo, and it has two distinct parts which are incoherent, if not downright inconsistent, one linking the god with Delphi, the other with Delos, his two most important centres. This example can be multiplied many times, as any modern handbook of Greek mythology reveals. The result was a considerable untidiness, to which another aspect of Greek religion contributed. Although all Greeks recognized and honoured the whole pantheon, no individual or community could conceivably perform all the rites to all of them. Each city had its patron deity and its special affinities with certain other gods and goddesses, who were accordingly celebrated even beyond Zeus himself, the unchallenged head of the pantheon, though no one denied Zeus's supremacy. Again there was the occasional sceptic, and again the people as a whole saw no difficulty.

Greek religion of the Archaic period was essentially a development from the basis already evident in the Homeric poems. By a variety of formalized actions, men sought to establish the most favourable possible relationships with the supernatural powers. That is to say, they tried to discover the will of the gods, and to placate and please them. The former required specialists, such as soothsayers, diviners and seers, but the rest of the activity was carried on by ordinary people, both privately, in their homes or through private associations, and publicly, by officials of the state. There were many officials called *hiereis*, a word which we translate as 'priests' despite the fact that they were normally laymen carrying on one particular public function exactly like all the other officials, civil and military. While kings still existed, they performed the state rites; now they were replaced by members of the aristocracy (and later by democratically chosen magistrates). And the rules were laid down without the intervention of a sanctified caste, backed only by tradition and myth. It was Homer and Hesiod, according to Herodotus (II 53), who 'first fixed for the Greeks the genealogy of the gods, gave the gods their titles, divided among them their honours and functions, and defined their images'. This may not be literally accurate but it points to the essential truth that in so far as the Greeks had an authority in these matters, it was largely the authority of poets, who may have claimed (and even believed) to be 'inspired by the Muses' but who cannot by any recognizable standard be equated with prophets or priests. Poetic inspiration is not prophetic revelation.

The activities through which the gods were honoured and supplicated included table fellowship (sharing food and drink with them), singing, dancing and processions, allowing oneself to be possessed (maenadism and other forms of 'orgiastic' behaviour), and games featuring feats of prowess (for physical excellence was as much the gift of the gods as anything else). Religion, in sum, was not set aside in a separate compartment but was meshed into every aspect of personal and social behaviour. What was not included was a theology or spiritual exercise, not even in the 'mystery religions', such as the cult of Demeter at Eleusis. These involved hereditary priesthoods and a sort of personal communion, but the activity was nevertheless still restricted to formalized words, rites and spectacles.

Of all the rites, sacrifice, both vegetable and animal, was the most universal—it is hard to think of any significant action which was not preceded by a sacrifice—and therefore the altar was the basic piece of equipment, with the hearth in the house also serving as one. Altars were found everywhere, in conjunction with secular public buildings, assembly-places and temples, at the city-gates, in the countryside at sacred places. Often a 'shrine' consisted of nothing more than a altar surrounded by a bit of marked out 'sacred ground'. Then, as the material level advanced towards the end of the Dark Age, the temple made its appearance in the eighth century. Though the temple had been common in the Near East for two thousand years, it had been so rare and insignificant in Bronze Age Greece that we may properly speak of it as an innovation now. Its function was not to serve as a house of worship, at least not normally, but to be the home of the god, where his statue was kept together with the treasure he accumulated through dedications from grateful mortals. The earliest temples were of wood and rubble or sun-dried brick and are known to us only from a few terracotta models, narrow one-roomed buildings with a simple porch at one end framed by two columns supporting the gable. The first stone temples were built about 600 B.C., and with them came the great leap to the large structures that were ever after the hallmark of ancient Greek architecture, the oblong room (or rooms), covered by a pitched roof and ringed by rows of columns, with the spaces between the column capitals and the roof decorated by sculpted reliefs. The earliest surviving remains of Doric temples are as widely scattered as Argos, Olympia, Delphi, Corcyra (Corfu) and Sicily; none of these is later than 550 B.C.

In the course of the Archaic period certain religious centres acquired pan-Hellenic status because they had something extraordinary to offer. One group consisted of shrines where particularly effective oracles could be consulted. The ability to foretell the future was a very specialized and valuable skill. Diviners who 'read' the flight of birds, dream interpreters, seers who had visions, were usually private persons able to persuade clients that their powers were real and legitimate. However, nothing in this field could rival the direct voice of a god, especially Apollo, who had special shrines for this purpose in various places in Hellas, with Delphi unchallenged in pre-eminence. In all but one respect Delphi was just another small Greek community, whose religious life was administered in the normal ways. When the shrine of Apollo became oracular is unknown, nor is the procedure clear to us. On stated days, inquirers who had performed the required sacrifices and rites of purification (and paid a considerable fee) were permitted to address themselves to the god, either on their own behalf or as agents of their communities. Apollo replied through a female medium called the Pythia or Pythoness, her utterances were transcribed into often ambiguous verses by the chief priest, a lay official, and the inquirer then had to put the best interpretation on them he could. There was thus a mystical element at Delphi setting it apart from the usual rituals, though not from those at other oracle-shrines, each of which had its own particular method of operation. Most puzzling is the role of a woman as the god's mouthpiece, an uncommon practice among oracles, the singularity of which is further highlighted by the fact that all other women were denied admission to the temple.

The triumph of Delphi is evident not only from the many oracles mentioned or quoted by Greek writers and from the vast complex of 'treasure-houses', temples and statuary that grew up in the sacred precinct, but also from the way Delphic activity was retrospectively backdated to a time when the shrine was certainly still only local in its importance. We have seen in Chapter 8 that not a few of the traditions about the consultation of Delphi in the foundation of early colonies were probably later inventions. It was in the seventh century, rather than the eighth, that Delphi was elevated to the greatest of the pan-Hellenic oracles. Although Greeks eventually travelled great distances to consult Apollo at Didyma near Miletus and at Claros in Asia Minor, or Zeus at Dodona in Epirus and at Siwa in Libya—to name a few main oracles—no other centre rivalled Delphi.

Delphi also organized games which acquired pan-Hellenic status, as did the temples at Nemea and Isthmia near Corinth. But in this field none could equal the quadrennial games in honour of Zeus at Olympia. The traditional date of their foundation is 776 B.C., which may well be exact and would give us the first fixed date in Greek history. Again the evidence suggests that at first the Olympic games attracted chiefly Peloponnesian Greeks, only later gathering momentum and drawing participants and spectators from all Hellas. In time the games programmes became very elaborate, including competitions in poetry, music and dance as well as public recitations and orations, but the main attraction (at Olympia the only one) was always in the athletics, chariot-racing, boxing and wrestling.

It was, then, in their cult activites, and in the poetry, architecture, sculpture and athletics associated with them, that the politically fragmented and often warring Greeks came closest to achieving some sort of unity in action. However, their religion was not a great force for *political* unity or even for peace within Hellas. Apollo was often consulted at Delphi before a war was undertaken, and it is not on record that he ever recommended peace as a good in itself, though he sometimes advised against a particular venture on its merits. The festivals themselves were times of limited truce, but their contribution over the long term to peace, or even to good will among the communities, does not seem to have been very tangible.

The origins of the practice of featuring athletic contests at important religious occasions are lost in the Dark Age.

The elaborate account in the twenty-third book of the *Iliad* of the games organized by Achilles for the funeral of Patroclus is our earliest literary evidence, and it already reveals something of the complicated psychology involved. The Greek word we translate as 'contest' is *agon*, and ultimately its range of meanings included not only an athletic or poetical contest but also a lawsuit, a battle, a crisis or deep anxiety (hence our word 'agony'). In the present context, *agon* is best left untranslated; the *agon* was the outstanding, ritualized, non-military expression of a value system in which honour was the highest virtue, for which one strove even at the cost of one's life, and in which loss of honour, shame, was the most intolerable disaster that could befall a man. Honour-and-shame cultures have existed (and still exist) in other societies, as among the Bedouins or in Balkan and Mediterranean districts, and the values and attitudes can probably be found in some measure in every society. What stands out among the ancient Greeks is the intensity with which these values were pursued at the religious festivals. The greatest literary formulation, and also the latest to retain so much archaic traditionalism, will be found in the poems of Pindar, who died about 438 B.C. At a time when Athens was in the full bloom of its democratic culture, Pindar was still celebrating the victors at the games not only by singing their praises but also by gloating brutally over the defeated and their crushing dishonour:

And now four times you came down with bodies beneath you,
—You meant them harm—
To whom the Pythian feast has given
No glad home-coming like yours.
They, when they meet their mothers,
Have no sweet laughter around them, moving delight.
In back streets, out of their enemies' way,
They cower; for disaster has bitten them.

(*Pythian* VIII 81–7)[1]

Pindar's values were largely those of the archaic

[1] Translated by C. M. Bowra, *Pindar* (Oxford, Clarendon Press; New York, Oxford University Press, 1964), p. 183.

aristocracy, with whom the *agon* was intimately associated. Of all victories, the highest honour was achieved in the chariot race, the most expensive of sports, the one, therefore, that tyrants aimed for in particular. Pindar and other specialists in the epinician odes, as the poems in praise of the victors were called, put their art at the disposal of tyrants as freely as of other aristocrats. That is one way they revealed their rejection of the new social and political values which were appearing in the later Archaic age. Another was their total immersion in myth. If, however, we compare these odes with the *Iliad*'s account of the funeral games for Patroclus, an important new tone can be heard. Homer celebrates individual heroes, whereas in the odes the victors are linked not only with their ancestry and kin but also with their communities in the honour that has come to them. In short, in the archaic *agon* there emerges that dialogue, and ultimately that tension, between individual and community which has been an element in western society ever since.

Given the nature of our evidence, we know nothing about the attitudes of ordinary people to the values Pindar was still expressing, though there can be little doubt that the games attracted all sections of the population as spectators. Yet opposition to the aristocratic ethos was inevitable, on the one hand among moralists who began to move beyond the honour-shame syndrome, on the other hand among those who were engaged in the long struggle to break the aristocratic monopoly of wealth and power. Taming the Homeric kind of hero was not enough; it was also necessary to damp down the spirit of the *agon*, if not to destroy it altogether, as a negative and even disruptive factor within the community. We can see this clearly in the poems of Solon, respecter of the rights of the upper classes though he was. Even war, it should be added, had become a community affair and could no longer, with the coming of the hoplite phalanx, be conducted in the spirit of the *agon*.

The tension between the individual and public authority is already sharply expressed in the *Works and Days* of Hesiod. Although the language and metre of the poem are in the epic tradition and it retains strong mythical elements, the *Works and Days* is a 'private' poem, written in the first person. It is also one of the blackest lamentations ever composed, filled with horror at the 'iron age' of poverty and injustice in which men now live, bitter against the 'gift-devouring judges', against the dangers of idleness and luxury and the ever present threat of poverty, an attitude which is all the more remarkable when one notes that the 'I' of the poem is both a bard, at least semi-professionally, and a farmer rich enough to own slaves and to look ahead to acquiring still more land by the fruits of his toil.

Two fundamentally new elements were thus introduced into Greek poetry, to remain dominant to the end of the Archaic period, though not necessarily always in combination as in the *Works and Days*. One was the personal element, the poet speaking in his own name. Although it may be a mistake to draw the inference automatically that he was therefore always being autobiographical, rather than merely employing an accepted convention that poetry is to be written in the first person, the poems nevertheless reveal 'what standpoints he wished to adopt, what emotions he preferred to express, and what topics he preferred to develop'.[1]

The topics often included social and political criticism, as with the Spartan Tyrtaeus, Solon, Alcaeus of Lesbos or Theognis of Megara, and that is the second new element. This criticism was by no means all in one direction. One will find in the collection of elegiac verses attributed to Theognis, for example, a very different point of view and different overtones with respect to the aristocracy from those we have seen in Solon:

> In rams and asses and horses, Cyrnus, we seek thoroughbreds ... but a noble man does not mind marrying the bad daughter of a bad sire if he gives much wealth, nor does a woman spurn to be bed-mate of a bad but rich man, for she would rather be rich than good. ... The breed is mongrelized by riches.
>
> (lines 183–91)

[1] K. J. Dover in *Entretiens sur l'antiquité classique*, vol. 10, *Archiloque* (Vandœuvres-Genève, Fondation Hardt, 1963), p. 212.

Never does slavery grow straight of head, but is always crooked and holds her neck askew. The child of a slave-woman never has the quality of the free-born, any more than a rose or a hyacinth grows on a squill.

(lines 535–8)

The variety of ideas and standpoints reflects both the new 'individualism' and the growing complexity of, and conflicts within, the social situation. It also marks the emergence of rudimentary moral and political concepts. Poets and philosophers began, in this unsystematic fashion, to examine, and to argue about, the nature of justice, wealth, human inequality, rights and moral duties. In their own way they were looking abstractly at the problems that their fellow-Greeks were facing in the hard world of power struggles, of law reform and *stasis* and tyranny, and eventually of democracy.

The new poetry had to break not only from the heroic outlook but also from the heroic or epic style (which the poets knew very well and which they continued to echo freely). New metres were created and poems became much shorter.[1] Often the poems were also personal in the narrow sense that they abandoned the larger social canvas and concentrated on love, the delights of wine, friendship and revelry. These developments are already visible in the earliest of the new-style poets whose work survives in any quantity (though even then mostly in fragments), Archilochus of Paros, whose mature work may be dated rather precisely to 650 or 640 B.C. The variety of his metrical forms indicates that behind him there lay a long experience in popular song, which co-existed with the epic tradition. This kind of poetry the world over is customarily linked with an occasion, whether a drinking-party, a village harvest dance or a great public festival, and more often than not it is also linked with song. (The very word 'lyric' implies that the poems were sung or chanted to an accompaniment on the lyre.) The occasion helped determine not only the style and subject-matter but also the conventions

---

[1] The *Works and Days* was still more than 800 lines in length, at least in the text that has come down to us, the *Theogony* half as long again.

appropriate to particular kinds of poetry. None of this is very clear in the fragments of Archilochus, but it cannot be doubted for most of the lyricists who followed, ranging as they did in seriousness from the drinking-songs of Anacreon to the great choral odes of Pindar and his predecessors.

The writers of choral odes, in particular, travelled widely in the Greek world in search of patrons, but many of the other poets were fairly mobile as well. Archaic poetry was thus truly pan-Hellenic, and it is noteworthy that the poets themselves originated not only on the mainland of Greece and the Aegean islands, but also in Asia Minor and the newer centres of the west. When we turn to a quite different intellectual development, the rise of philosophy about 600 B.C., Old Greece appears to have played no role at all in the first phase. The beginning was in Ionia, and particularly in Miletus, and then, in the latter half of the sixth century, a second centre developed in Sicily and southern Italy, apparently inspired by political refugees. Xenophanes fled from Colophon to Sicily about the middle of the century, Pythagoras a bit later from Samos to Croton, where he seems to have founded a genuine school, which was at the same time a secret mystical sect.

One cannot avoid the word 'seems' in discussing these early 'physicists', as the Greeks called them from *physis* (nature), because the traditions that have come down to us about them are fragmentary, confused and in large part untrustworthy. However, whatever the truth may be about the details, there can be no disputing the revolution in thought they initiated, summed up in the familiar phrase, from myth to *logos* or reason. For a considerable time the revolution lay in the mode of thinking rather than in the answers given, which were speculative, and, in the light of later knowledge, often naïve in the extreme. Indeed, such questions as, What was in the beginning?, were not really new. But the answers had hitherto been mythical ones, specific and concrete, explaining both natural and human phenomena by reciting particular supernatural events or actions, in themselves unaccountable. 'Myth was a narrative, not the solution of a problem.... The

problem found itself resolved without having been posed.'[1]
The Ionian revolution, then, was simply that they posed
problems and proposed general, rational, 'impersonal'
answers.

How could the human species have survived in the
beginning, given the long period during which the human
infant is helpless? There is a genuine problem, posed by
Anaximander of Miletus early in the sixth century. 'He
says,' a late writer tells us, 'that in the beginning man was
born from creatures of a different kind; because other creatures are soon self-supporting, but man alone needs prolonged nursing. For this reason he would not have survived
if this had been his original form.' Details are added by
another late writer: 'Anaximander of Miletus conceived
that there arose from heated water and earth either fish or
creatures very like fish; in these men grew, in the form of
embryos retained within until puberty; then at last the
fish-like creatures burst and men and women who were
already able to nourish themselves stepped forth.'[2] Naïve
as this speculation may be, it is nevertheless separated by a
wide gulf from Hesiod's mythical account (*Works and Days*
60–82) of the creation of woman:

> And he [Zeus] bade famous Hephaestus make haste and
> mix earth with water and to put in it the voice and strength of
> human kind, and fashion a sweet, lovely maiden-shape, like to
> the immortal goddesses in face; and Athena to teach her nee-
> dlework and the weaving of the varied web; and golden Aphro-
> dite to shed grace upon her head and cruel longing and cares
> that weary the limb. And he charged Hermes the guide, the
> slayer of Argus, to put in her a shameless mind and deceitful
> nature.... And he called this woman Pandora, because all
> they who dwelt on Olympus gave each a gift, a plague to men
> who eat bread.[3]

[1] J.-P. Vernant, *Mythe et pensée chez les grecs* (Paris, Maspero, 1965), p. 291.

[2] Translated in G.S. Kirk and J. E. Raven, *The Presocratic Philosophers. A Critical History with a Selection of Texts* (Cambridge and New York, Cambridge University Press, 1962), p. 141.

[3] Translated by H.G. Evelyn-White in the Loeb Classical Library (Cambridge, Mass., Harvard University Press; London, Heinemann).

That is a mythical explanation of the existence of evil, a problem Hesiod never actually posed as such. The revolution of the Ionian physicists, with their assumption of the existence of regularities in nature, and hence of the possibility of generalized explanations, subject to rational discovery and to rational argument and debate, in which they engaged freely, was therefore a necessary prerequisite for both philosophy and science (as distinct from merely empirical knowledge, for example, in metallurgy and navigation, of which the Greeks by now possessed a considerable stock). That is their importance, rather than the particular theories attributed to them. And behind them, as an immediate stimulant to their new approach, lay the practice of rational debate, free from supernatural interference and against the hitherto unarguable claims of aristocratic tradition, that was developing within the emergent *polis* in the social and political spheres.

The earlier Ionians seem to have concentrated their efforts largely on the cosmos and the nature of being generally. But Xenophanes, at least, was more of a moralist, and even a theologian; some of his famous aphorisms were radical and biting: 'Homer and Hesiod have attributed to the gods everything that is a shame and reproach among men, stealing and committing adultery and deceiving each other' (Kirk and Raven, p. 168). And the Pythagoreans turned their attention to the soul and elaborated a doctrine of transmigration and re-incarnation. Their mystical doctrine somehow—though all this is now hopelessly obscure—drew them into the complicated politics of the Greek cities in southern Italy, where they became centres of faction and revolution. Thereafter Greek philosophy was to manifest an intense concern with, and involvement in, the actual life of the community, its politics and its social and ethical behaviour. One thinks especially of Socrates and Plato, of Aristotle or the later Stoics.

Finally, the history of the visual arts, too, is a counterpoint on the themes that have run through this chapter. Despite the many regional and local variations, the arts were pan-Hellenic, as evidenced not only by the ease with which sculptors and architects travelled—and their ideas as well—but also by the total impact. A seventh- or sixth-century Greek found himself in a relatively familiar environment, in this respect, wherever he went. Art, like poetry, was directly or indirectly functional; its canons were closely tied to its purposes. Art was meshed in with daily living, not set apart for occasional leisure time or for the enjoyment of rich collectors and aesthetes. It was found in the temples and other public buildings, not in museums. In the homes, there were beautiful vases, mirrors and jewelry rather than *objets d'art*. Even in the most private of the arts one rarely finds among the innumerable vases, pitchers and cups a non-functional, eccentric object.

By the sixth century potters, painters and sculptors began the practice of signing some of their works, a revolutionary step in the history of art, proclaiming the recognition of the artist as an individual (exactly like the lyric poet). Yet he did not become a rampant individualist, restlessly seeking novelty. In any given period and place he worked within the recognized canons (and his clients did not demand otherwise), placing his individual stamp on his output within that framework. Of course, in the continuous history of fine painted pottery, which goes back uninterruptedly to the beginning of the Dark Age, there were great changes not only in technique but also in fashion and taste. The most remarkable of all, perhaps, was the capture of the market in much of the Greek world, most notably in the west, by Athenian ware about the middle of the sixth century. The existence of canons and rules did not lead to mechanical repetition and sterility. Viewing the history of the potter's art whole, one therefore sees an effective interplay between the artist as individual and the artist as functionary or spokesman of his society.

The other visual arts have a much shorter history so far as our knowledge goes. Almost all painting from this period other than on pottery is lost, and architecture and sculpture are known in detail only from the time when stone, bronze and terracotta began to be employed in place of perishable wood and sun-dried brick, that is, from the seventh century B.C. What then strikes us forcibly is how heavily dominated these arts were by religious contexts and purposes. Greek architecture and sculpture were public arts in the strict sense. Archaic (and classical) Greece was a world without palaces or private mansions. Among public buildings, furthermore, the greatest effort and expenditure were lavished on temples. They were often decorated with sculptured metopes, pediments and friezes, and they housed statues of the gods to whom they were dedicated. Outside the temple, too, the connexion of sculpture with religion was more common than may at first sight seem the case. Statues of the victors in the great games come into this category: like the choral odes, these statues were a form of thanksgiving by the community (or tyrant) whom the athletes represented. Like the odes, too, the statues were not really concerned with the athletes as individuals; they were not portraits but ideal types, employed indiscriminately for men and gods. The familiar archaic statues of young nude males (*kouroi*) in stone or bronze, of which more than two hundred are now known beginning about 650 B.C., are sometimes labelled 'Apollo' by modern scholars and sometimes 'Youth'. But the distinction between god and man is legitimate only when there is external evidence, if the statue is funerary, for example, or if the base survives with an inscribed text. There is nothing in the statue itself from which to tell.

Such sculpture, like the temple, symbolized the triumph of the community, a demonstration of its growing strength and self-consciousness. Mycenaean rulers erected great palaces and tombs for themselves. Not until the age of tyranny were there again individuals in Greece who commanded enough power and resources to emulate them. Yet even tyrants did not customarily build palaces or splendid tombs in self-glorification. Peisistratus may have lived on the Acropolis for a time, but his 'memorial' there was not a palace but the temple of Athena Parthenos. This, like his Fountain-House, a complex structure, probably at the southwestern corner of the agora, which was a major feature of the city's water-supply system, reveals how far the Greek community had advanced as a living force, so that even a tyrant bowed to it. Homer's heroes lived on in the tales of their feats of prowess. The new 'heroes' immortalized themselves in public buildings.

In all this cultural history there were many Near Eastern sources and influences, on myth, in mathematics, temple-building and sculpture, pottery decoration. If nothing has been said about that here, that is not from any desire to deny the existence of these influences but with the intention of getting the balance right. Whatever the Greeks borrowed they promptly absorbed and converted into something original in so far as anything other than technique (in metallurgy, for example) was involved. They borrowed the Phoenician alphabet, but there were no Phoenician Homers. The idea of the free-standing human statue may have come to them from Egypt (though that common view has been challenged),[1] but it was the Greeks, not the Egyptians, who then developed the idea, from the archaic *kouroi* and the female *korai* on to the great classical statuary. In the process they not only invented the nude as an art-form but, in a very important sense, they 'invented art' itself. 'It was the Greeks who taught us to ask "*How* does he stand?" or even "Why does he stand like that?"'[2] It is not far-fetched to associate such questions, which, of course, we do not know that any early Greek sculptor actually put to himself, with the kinds of questions the physicists were asking at the same time. The human self-reliance and self-confidence that permitted and fostered such questions, in politics as in art and philosophy, lay at the root of the *miracle grec*.

---

[1] R. M. Cook, 'Origins of Greek Sculpture', *Journal of Hellenic Studies*, 87 (1967), pp. 24–32.
[2] E. H. Gombrich, *Art and Illusion* (rev. ed., London, Phaidon; Princeton University Press, 1962), pp. 114, 120.

Select English Bibliography

Introductory note: Books and articles mentioned in the footnotes are not repeated here. Full excavation reports have not been included; preference has been given to the more general summaries, when possible to the most recent, which usually contain good bibliographies.

As a general introduction to the study of early societies, V. Gordon Childe, *Man Makes Himself* (4 ed., London, Watts, 1965; New York, New American Library, 1952), has become a classic.

The relevant volumes (I and II) of the *Cambridge Ancient History* have been completely rewritten and published in two parts each (3 ed., 1970–75). A few individual chapters are cited below in an abbreviated reference: *CAH* followed by volume and chapter number.

THE BRONZE AGE

The best synoptic account is now J. M. Coles and A. F. Harding, *The Bronze Age in Europe* (London, Methuen, 1979); of Greece (excluding Crete), Emily Vermeule, *Greece in the Bronze Age* (University of Chicago Press, 1964). The best illustrated work is F. Matz, *Crete and Early Greece* (London, Methuen, 1962), though special note must be taken of Max Hirmer's photographs in S. Marinatos and M. Hirmer, *Crete and Mycenae* (London, Thames & Hudson; New York, Abrams, 1960).

On the complex and vital question of metal resources, see J. D. Muhly, 'Copper and Tin. The Distribution of Mineral Resources and the Nature of the Metals Trade in the Bronze Age', *Transactions of the Connecticut Academy of Arts and Sciences*, 43 (1973), pp. 155–535, with supplement in vol. 46 (1976), pp. 77–136. A. Snodgrass, *Early Greek Armour and Weapons* (Edinburgh University Press; Chicago, Aldine Publishing Co., 1964), carries his detailed inquiry into the Dark Age. B. Rutkowski, *Cult Places in the Aegean World* (Polish Academy of Sciences, 1972), replaces all

BIBLIOGRAPHY

previous accounts and is notable for its sobriety. For a subtle and complex study of the art which, despite the title, extends to Bronze Age Greece and Crete, see H. A. Groenewegen-Frankfort, *Arrest and Movement. An Essay on Space and Time in the Representational Art of the Ancient Near East* (London, Faber; New York, Humanities Press, 1951), summarized in simplified form in *The Ancient World*, written in collaboration with B. Ashmole, volume I of the paperback series, *The Library of Art History* (Mentor Books, 1967).

On the archaeological and linguistic analyses by which the attempt has been made to pinpoint and explain the 'coming of the Greeks', see the following chapters in *CAH:* I 26(a), 27; II 39(a); also John Chadwick, *The Decipherment of Linear B* (Cambridge University Press, 1968). O. Gurney, *The Hittites* (Penguin, repr. 1976), is relevant on this and other topics in Greek History.

On the Cyclades, see C. Renfrew, *The Emergence of Civilization: The Cyclades and the Aegean in the Third Millennium B.C.* (London, Methuen, 1972), and 'The Development and Chronology of the Early Cycladic Figures', *American Journal of Archaeology*, 73 (1969), pp. 1–32; *Papers in Cycladic Prehistory*, ed. J. L. Davis and J. F. Cherry (Institute of Archaeology, University of California, Los Angeles, Monograph XIV, 1979). On Cyprus, see the chapters in *CAH* by H. W. Catling: *p* 9(c), 26(b); II 4(c), 22(b).

Sinclair Hood, *The Minoans* (London, Thames & Hudson; New York, Praeger, 1974), and R. W. Hutchinson, *Prehistoric Crete* (Penguin, 1962), provide good general surveys. J. D. S. Pendlebury, *The Archaeology of Crete* (London, Methuen, 1939; New York, Norton paperback, 1965) remains important though antiquated. J. W. Graham, *The Palaces of Crete* (Princeton University Press, 1962), is the standard work. A brief account of the 'rediscovery of Crete' will be found in M. I. Finley, *Aspects of Antiquity* (2 ed., Penguin, 1977), ch. 1. On special topics: J. D. Evans, 'Neolithic Knossos: the Growth of a Settlement', *Proceedings of the Prehistoric Society*, 37 (1971) II, pp. 95–117; J. T. Killen, 'The Wool Industry of Crete in the Late Bronze Age', *Annual of the British School at Athens*, 59 (1964), pp. 1–15; M. R. Popham, *The Destruction of the Palace at Knossos* (Lund, 1970).

J. T. Hooker, *Mycenaean Greece* (London and Boston, Routledge and Kegan Paul, 1976), provides the best introduction.

BIBLIOGRAPHY

THE ARCHAIC AGE

A. M. Snodgrass, *The Dark Age of Greece* (Edinburgh University Press, 1971), replaces all previous books on the subject. The best 'narrative' remains C. G. Starr, *The Origins of Greek Civilization, 1100–650 B.C.* (New York, Knopf, 1961; London, Jonathan Cape, 1962). For a detailed history after the Dark Age, see A. R. Burn, *The Lyric Age of Greece* (London, Arnold; New York, St. Martin's and Funk & Wagnalls, 1960). A lively, though uneven, account of the period from the end of the Dark Age to the close of the Persian wars, with extensive quotation from Greek literature and inscriptions, is provided by O. Murray, *Early Greece* (Fontana Paperbacks, 1980).

The best balanced account of Homer and the 'Homeric problem' is G. S. Kirk, *The Songs of Homer* (Cambridge University Press, 1962), also issued in a shortened paperback version as *Homer and the Epic* (1965). For an attempt to reconstruct Dark Age society from the poems, see M. I. Finley, *The World of Odysseus* (rev. ed., New York, Viking Press; London, Chatto & Windus, 1978), with an appendix on Schliemann and Troy. See further Finley, *Economy and Society in Ancient Greece*, ed. B. D. Shaw and R. P. Saller (London, Chatto & Windus; New York, Viking Press, 1981), ch. 12–14, for an examination of the radical differences in economic and social institutions between the Mycenaean and 'Homeric' worlds. The basic introductory account of the archaeology of Troy is C. W. Blegen, *Troy and the Trojans* (London, Thames & Hudson; New York, Praeger, 1963). The present state of the debate over the historicity of the traditional account is brought into sharp focus by M. I. Finley, 'The Trojan War', with replies by J. L. Caskey, G. S. Kirk and D. L. Page, *Journal of Hellenic Studies*, 84 (1964), pp. 1–20; see also Finley, *Aspects of Antiquity*, already mentioned above.

On 'colonization', see John Boardman, *The Greeks Overseas* (2 ed., Penguin, 1973); T. J. Dunbabin, *The Western Greeks* (Oxford University Press, 1948), though often out of date archaeologically; M. I. Finley, *Ancient Sicily* (rev. ed., London, Chatto & Windus, 1979), ch. 1–3; J. M. Cook, 'Greek Settlement in the Eastern Aegean and Asia Minor', *CAH* II 38; R. D. Barnett, 'Phrygia and the Peoples of Anatolia in the Iron Age', *CAH* II 30; M. M. Austin, *Greece and Egypt in the Archaic Age* (*Proceedings of the*

BIBLIOGRAPHY

Cambridge Philological Society, Supp. no. 2, 1970).

A. Andrewes, *The Greek Tyrants* (London, Hutchinson; New York, Harper & Row paperback, 1956), remains the standard introduction in English. On Archaic Sparta and Athens, see P. Cartledge, *Sparta and Lakonia. A Regional History 1300–362 B.C.* (London and Boston, Routledge & Kegan Paul, 1979), parts I–II; V. Ehrenberg, *From Solon to Socrates* (2 ed., London, Methuen, 1973).

On various aspects of Archaic culture, the following titles are self-explanatory: P. A. L. Greenhalgh, *Early Greek Warfare* (Cambridge University Press, 1973); G. S. Kirk, *The Nature of Greek Myths* (Penguin, 1974); H. W. Parke and D. E. Wormell, *The Delphic Oracle* (2 vols. Oxford, Blackwell; New York, Humanities Press, 1956); W. K. C. Guthrie, *A History of Greek Philosophy*, vol. I (Cambridge University Press, 1962); G. E. R. Lloyd, *Early Greek Science: Thales to Aristotle* (London, Chatto & Windus; New York, Norton, 1970), ch. 1–3, and *Magic, Reason and Experience* (Cambridge University Press, 1979); A. W. H. Adkins, *Merit and Responsibility. A Study in Greek Values* (Oxford University Press, 1962), ch. 1–8; L. H. Jeffery, *The Local Scripts of Archaic Greece* (Oxford University Press, 1961); C. M. Bowra, *Greek Lyric Poetry from Alcman to Simonides* (2 ed., Oxford University Press, 1961); M. Robertson, *A History of Greek Art* (2 vols., Cambridge University Press, 1975), ch. 1–3; R. M. Cook, *Greek Painted Pottery* (2 ed., London, Methuen; New York, Barnes & Noble, 1972); J. N. Coldstream, *Greek Geometric Pottery* (London, Methuen; New York, Barnes & Noble, 1968); A. M. Snodgrass, 'Poet and Painter in Eighth-Century Greece', *Proceedings of the Cambridge Philological Society*, n.s. 25 (1979), pp. 118–30. Perhaps half the essays in Bruno Snell, *The Discovery of the Mind*, translated by T. G. Rosenmeyer (Oxford, Blackwell; New York, Harper & Row, 1953), deal with Archaic ideas and literature.

A note on sources: Apart from the two Homeric poems, available in a variety of editions and translations, and the poetry of Hesiod, excellently rendered into prose by H. G. Evelyn-White in the *Loeb Classical Library* edition, contemporary written sources are restricted to fragments of the poets and philosphers. The former are collected in five Loeb volumes, entitled *Lyra Graeca* and *Elegy and Iambus*, edited by J. M. Edmonds, but the reader must be warned that the editor exercised a free hand in reconstructing and rendering the fragments. There is an excellent selection of the philosophical fragments, in the original and translation, with full discussion, in G. S. Kirk and J. E. Raven, *The Presocratic Philosophers* (Cambridge Unversity Press, 1962).

Index

INDEX

INDEX